D1827037

Teaching Literature in the Language Classroom

by Jennifer Hill

Essential Language Teaching Series

General Editors: Monica Vincent

Roger H. Flavell

First published 1986

Published by *Macmillan Publishers Ltd*
London and Basingstoke
Associated companies and representatives in Accra,
Auckland, Delhi, Dublin, Gaborone, Harare,
Hong Kong, Kuala Lumpur, Lagos, Manzini, Melbourne,
Mexico City, Nairobi, New York, Singapore, Tokyo

ISBN 0–333–42389–5

Hill, Jennifer
    Teaching literature in the classroom.—
    (Essential language teaching series)
    1. English language—Study and teaching—
    Foreign students   2. English literature—
    Study and teaching
    I. Title   II. Series
    428.2′4′ 07   PE1128.A2
    ISBN 0–333–42389–5

Acknowledgements

My very grateful thanks to Jean-Claude Albus, at Abidjan University, to John Spencer, formerly of Leeds University and whose idea this book was and to Monica Vincent for their help and advice. Above all I would like to thank my husband, for his patience and encouragement.

Author's Note

While this book covers the field of literature generally I have concentrated on the novel in particular as an area which has received little attention recently.

I have tried not to assume the reader's familiarity with any of the texts which I have used as examples of literary technique. It would undoubtedly be helpful to readers, however, to have their own copy of those referred to most frequently:

Animal Farm George Orwell
Flowers for Mrs Harris Paul Gallico
Lord of the Flies William Golding
Oliver Twist Charles Dickens
The Bridge of San Luis Rey Thornton Wilder
The Rover Joseph Conrad
Things Fall Apart Chinua Achebe
Typhoon Joseph Conrad

Dedicated to
a great artist, Eleane Bonsell,
in memory of
the silver buttons

Contents

1 Why teach literature?

It is said that the study of literature 'begins in delight and ends in wisdom' and this is as true for an EFL/ESL student of English as it is for a native speaker. Over the past few decades there has, however, been much discussion of the value of trying to teach any kind of literature, whether the classics or merely any imaginative work written in English, as part of an EFL/ESL syllabus. In the sixties and seventies, in fact, there was a distinct reaction against the use of any literary English at all in the classroom, but now the pendulum has swung the other way and there is a renewed interest in literature teaching.

1.1 The case for literature

The many 'educational' arguments put forward in the past for including literature are, of course, still valid, both in terms of its contribution to the students' general knowledge and to their intellectual, social and moral development, as well as of its universal appeal to the emotions.

There are also good psychological and linguistic reasons for teaching literature. Extensive reading provides:
- the possibility of internalising the language and reinforcing points previously learned
- a genuine language context and a focal point for the students in their own efforts to communicate
- motivation.

Literature study can also provide a range of texts and an introduction to the many different varieties of English.

1.1.1 *Internalisation*

When people learn their native language they are not 'taught' the rules of grammar and the meaning of words; they work out how the language works from what they hear, imperfect though this sometimes is, and so internalise or construct mentally their knowledge of the language (Cairns and Cairns 1976: 216–220). Native speakers apparently learn the meaning of about 90 per cent of the words they know from meeting them in context and not from the dictionary. When confronted with an unknown word they are more likely to make an informed guess at its meaning, based perhaps on its linguistic context or what is going on round about them, than to look it up (Fowler 1971).

But how can foreign learners do this? In order to internalise the grammar and work out the meaning of words from their context, they must have a sufficiently large body of authentic and understandable material to work from, material Krashen calls 'comprehensible input' (Krashen 1985). It is plain that extensive reading will assist learners in this respect. ASstudy of a variety of texts, says Enkvist in *Linguistics and Style*, 'will provide a short-cut to the extensive experience of linguistic items in context that native speakers acquire by direct exposure'. (Enkvist, Spencer and Gregory 1964:5). Students thus substitute imaginary for real experience.

Such exposure to large amounts of authentic material will, moreover, reinforce what the students have previously studied as an academic exercise. The structures and vocabulary will subconsciously register and concepts already known will be reinforced by their discovery in a different context. Students become aware of the wider areas covered by a certain word, of its function in phrase and sentence, of the words with which it is usually associated, and all without conscious attention as they enjoy the book.

1.1.2 *A genuine context*

> Why is a story easier to remember than a collection of unrelated
> items?

Studies of the way in which people analyse and understand language have shown that the discourse context is very important. People analyse incoming messages in two ways: not only do they have information relative to certain collections of sounds and symbols stored in their memory, but they also have their own knowledge of the world and the context of the message to work from. They use that information to make predictions and inferences about what they hear or read and to assign particular 'meanings' to the 'data'. They thus actively contribute to the meaning of the message (Lindsay and Norman 1977).

The system of teaching languages which consists of setting isolated sentences to illustrate particular language points prevents the learners from making any analysis on the basis of context. They cannot participate in the meaning. Even native speakers have difficulty remembering unrelated words and structures and the problem is more acute for foreign learners (R J Riding 1977:76–78). They need a meaningful context to work from and to which they can relate what they learn, and an interesting text can supply that need.

Such a text would also supply a focal point for the students in their own efforts to communicate. One of the first requirements when trying to encourage students to take part in a conversation is clearly that they should have something important to say. They cannot 'communicate' in a vacuum, and the informational content of most situational dialogues is often insufficient to spur them to the difficult task of creating new sentences. Widdowson comments:

It's not easy to see how learners at any level can get interested in and therefore motivated by a dialogue about buying stamps at a post office. There is no plot, there is no mystery, there is no character; everything proceeds as if communication never created a problem. There's no misunderstanding and there's no possibility of any kind of interaction (Widdowson 1983).

Literature, on the other hand, is more likely to provide the necessary stimulus to incite students to speech.

1.1.3 *Motivation*

This brings us naturally to the question of motivation, perhaps the most important justification for including literature on the syllabus. Wilhelm von Humboldt said many years ago that we cannot teach language; we can only create conditions under which it can be learned. The importance of motivation in conditions relevant to the learning process cannot be stressed sufficiently. Literature provides not only a genuine context for com munication; it also give pleasure by engaging the emotions. As Reeves says:

If a reader wants to find out what happens next, if it seems important to him personally, he will read on despite linguistic difficulties (Reeves 1986).

Sometimes students need the added stimulus of an exciting story. Finding out just what *did* happen to the heroine may encourage them to read on when otherwise they may not.

1.2 Problems with literature

There are, however, distinct problems associated with the teaching of literature. It is, for example, common for 'classical' works to be included in a syllabus long before students are able to cope with them, and the over-reaction against the teaching literature referred to earlier was undoubtedly due in part to this. Other objections to the inclusion of literature were that it was ungradeable and linguistically unsuitable as a model and as the teaching of English for Specific Purposes increased, teachers often complained that the language of literature was irrelevant to their learners' needs.

1.2.1 Grading

Grading material allows learners to progress in small, regular steps and does not expose them to too much new material to cope with at any one time. Literature is difficult to grade for the following reasons:

- uncommon vocabulary (sometimes dated, specialised or archaic)
- complex syntax and structure (especially in poetry where, for example, abnormal word order is commonplace)
- lack of homogeneity (with different degrees of difficulty even within one text).

These factors obviously make it difficult to control the type of language to which the students are exposed.

The problem is not, however, insuperable. It is true that literature is difficult to grade, but it is possible to achieve a kind of progression which makes allowances for the language difficulties of students in the early stages of a syllabus (see Chapter 2). Students can actually advance in their grasp of the language by trying to understand material that is a little beyond them. They must deduce the meaning from the context and thus actively participate in what they read. This is, in itself, a step in the learning process (Krashen 1985). Very tight grading is not, therefore, the only answer, although it is plain that the students must be able to work out what the text means for themselves.

1.2.2 A linguistic model

It was also argued at one time that any material given to the students should provide a model or pattern on which they could base their own production of the language. The disadvantages mentioned above also applied to literature as a model, making it unsuitable as a basis for *practice material*. Much was made of the very personal way in which great authors had used the language and the fact that the teacher was therefore obliged to instruct the students, 'The author puts it this way. *You* had better not.' It was therefore maintained that the only *literature* to be allowed to students was that which had been simplified to the point where they could use the language themselves.

Now while it is true that literature cannot usually be used as a model in that sense, it does provide examples of language 'in use'. The communicative approach to language teaching stresses that students should not only have a thorough grasp of the language system itself, but also be able to use it appropriately according to the situation. Teachers have always had the problem of how to introduce 'real life' into the classroom, how to make the students aware of all the potential situations in which language may vary? Literature can provide those communicative situations for them, always providing that texts in good, modern English are chosen. Such texts may exemplify:

- degrees of formality, ranging from slang to an extremely formal mode of speech.
- dialect contrasted with standard English
- different topics of fields of experience (a book may be a love story, autobiography or travelogue)
- different levels of diction (e.g. the literary language of poetry or the colloquial speech of a play by Pinter).

It is also the case that for some language learners the need for written communication may be more important than an ability to communicate orally. Literature provides a whole range of texts which may be useful to them: essays, letters and reports, as well as novels and short stories. In any one text students may find examples of:

- description
- instruction
- narrative
- argumentation.

Their exposure to such texts should assist them greatly in their feel for what sort of language is appropriate in any particular situation and should lead to an improved grasp of the communicative functions of the language (Widdowson and Davies 1974).

1.2.3 *Relevancy*

Literary English was also seen as language unlikely to be used in everyday life and not related to the language which the students would finally produce nor the roles they hoped to fill. As Strevens wrote:

His [the citizen's] aim. . .is to acquire some degree of practical command of the language, largely unrelated to the study and appreciation of literature. The objectives of language teaching are to enable the young citizen to use English. . .as a tool: as a vehicle for comprehension and communication; or as a window on the modern trans-national world of science, technology, entertainment, art or ideas, or for quite specific or restricted needs in his occupation (Strevens 1974).

This is a valid point. If teachers restrict their study of literature to nineteenth century novels and Shakespeare's plays then it is certain that the language will be largely irrelevant to the needs of most students. If, however, they use good modern prose as the basis for their course, or works by local authors in English, then much of the language will have value for the students and (an important point) the material will motivate them. There is no reason why students studying Mechanical Engineering should be forever restricted to such articles as 'Displacement and Angular Velocity in Roller Cam Operations'.

The objections raised to the use of literature do have a certain validity, however. It is difficult to find suitable texts for the initial stages of a literature course. More emphasis must be placed on the students' communicative competence and clearly students must have a reasonably good command of the language before they are plunged into a study of literary texts. Such points should be kept in mind by a teacher preparing a literature course.

1.3 Aims and objectives

Despite these problems, however, it is plain that there are many reasons for including literature on our syllabus, whether of an educational, psycholinguistic or linguistic nature. It should contribute, as Figure 1 below demonstrates, both to the development of the student as an individual and to his or her command of the language.

There are obviously many different teaching situations:
- general language courses at post-intermediate levels (either with or without 'official' literature components)
- literature components of exam preparation courses (eg the Cambridge First and Proficiency Certificates)
- full time literature degree courses at university
- the use of literary texts in ESP courses at various levels.

Whatever the course may be, however, extensive reading and reading related activities should be included in the syllabus at the earliest possible moment, with anything from a quarter to a third of the time allotted to them. Teachers in charge of ESP classes might prefer to consider extracts instead of whole texts, but some time should be spent in reading for pleasure (see Chapter 3).

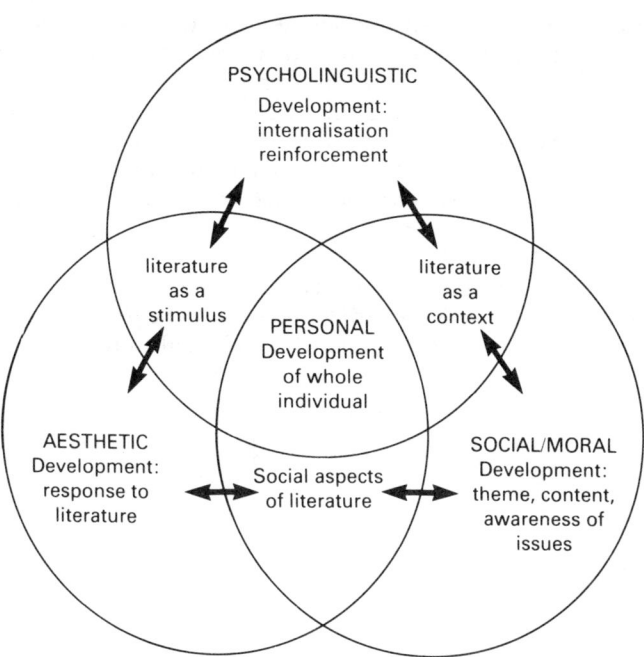

Figure 1 Based on *Best laid plans: English teachers at work,*
edited by Sue Horner

Literature which is going to be suitable for students, especially in the early stages of a language course, will have to be very carefully chosen indeed. Consider the classics of literature, by which is meant any text which has received both public and critical acclaim and which, generally speaking, has stood the test of time. They may well only be accessible to students at tertiary level (ie college or university), although there are a few which can be safely included earlier on. Students who take English language at the tertiary level are almost certainly going to have to consider literary texts and some preparation for this will be necessary.

Neil Gilroy-Scott, in his introduction to *Teaching Literature Overseas: Language-Based Approaches*, says:

There is an immediate need for guidance over the question of how to introduce students to the primary texts of literature. . .and how to teach them strategies and study habits to enable them to cope with the heavy reading requirements in most tertiary level courses (Gilroy-Scott 1983).

This book is therefore to help teachers decide which books to include and to suggest a variety of strategies to help students discover how language functions in a communicative way in those texts.

> *Warning*: The fact that literature may be a rich source of linguistic variety does not mean that teachers should turn each text into a set of language exercises of one sort or another. Remember we want the students to enjoy the work.

With an awareness of the potential for education enrichment which literature offers on a variety of levels, teachers can help students gain both pleasure and profit and delight and wisdom from their reading.

2 Choosing texts

The next point to consider is the selection of literary texts. Teachers of examination classes are obliged to choose from the texts prescribed by the examination board, but in other classes and in the area of supplementary reading there may be much more scope for individual choice of material. Ideally the development of reading skills will form part of the language course from the start, with students meeting texts of increasing complexity from the very simple up to the level required by a public examination. Teachers choosing texts, however, especially in the early stages of a syllabus, need to keep the following basic criteria in mind:

- the needs and abilities of the students
- the linguistic and stylistic level of the text
- the amount of background information required for a true appreciation of the material.

2.1 Student needs and abilities

2.1.1 *Age, interests and goals*
Although texts chosen for the early stages need to be fairly simple, they should be appropriate to the age, interests and goals of the students. Certain texts will appeal to younger children, others to teenagers, and it is a mistake to give adolescents material more suited to a younger child just because the language is simpler.

Such texts need not necessarily be 'Great Literature' as defined in Chapter 1, but they should be a 'good read'. Like Peter Dickinson's *The Seventh Raven*, an optional work set for the Cambridge First Certificate examination, they should have exciting plots and comprehensible characters. Good detective stories, science fiction and adventure stories are typical genres in modern fiction that appeal to young and old alike. There are also a variety of 'human interest' works which would be suitable for EFL/ESL students. Autobiographical works or travelogues might also be included (see Figure 2).

Poetry should be chosen for its immediate appeal. Many American authors (Robert Frost and Emily Dickinson, for example) have written works whose vocabulary and structure are quite appropriate for students in the early stages. Anthologies designed for secondary school children in Britain contain many suitable poems.

Any goals which students may have as the desired end result of their studies should also be borne in mind. Although a literary syllabus is certainly not chosen for its immediate 'usefulness', some texts are clearly more relevant for the foreign learner than others. Students are more likely to be motivated to read good modern prose and poetry since they will perceive such texts as better models for their own language production. Their often plain, straightforward language could conceivably be repro duced by students and avoid many of the linguistic, sociological and cultural barriers olders texts set up.

2.1.2 *The ability to read fluently*
In order to understand literary texts students need to be able to read at a reasonable speed and for an extended period without fatigue. This speed should, for extensive reading, be at a rate of at least 200 words per minute and up to 250 words or more, if possible. (When following a story, for example, good readers often read at a speed of 400 words per minute.) Many EFL/ESL students, however, especially those with a non-European first language, have reading speeds of only between 100 and 150 words a minute.

The ability to read at higher speeds is crucial to the students' understanding of the text overall; they must be able to see a passage as a complete unit, not just a collection of sentences with individual meanings. Students reading at the lower speeds common in EFL/ESL classes often lose the thread of the story and completely miss the point of any figurative language.

The reading speed of a class can be established roughly by timing page turning in sample students. A more accurate assessment can be made by timing an entire chapter and then checking comprehension by setting questions.

Because of the low average reading speed of EFL learners it is preferable to start with very short texts. Long passages of philosophising, description or irrelevant dialogue get in the way of the students' understanding. Such texts should be avoided. Short stories are an obvious choice at this stage and some short story anthologies designed for school use are listed in Figure 2 on page 18.

IMPROVING READING SPEED

Technical methods

Use a device of some kind to cover up the words as the students read:

- a travelling shade which progressively covers the words just read so that the student is unable to regress
- a mask to move over the page which covers over a third or half of a line at a time, forcing the student to guess at what is hidden
- a mask to cover over the words at a fixed speed on an overhead projector as the text is being projected onto the screen.

Practice methods

(1) Set a series of texts of similar length and complexity, followed by comprehension questions and slowly decrease the time allowed for reading each successive text.

(2) Provide the class with sets of graded readers for them to read as quickly as they can but at their own pace.

For a fuller discussion on reading speed see *Reading in the Language Classroom* (Williams 1984) and *Practical Faster Reading* (Mosback G and Mosback V 1976).

How many really short works of literature can you think of that are suitable for the EFL learner at the start of a course?

Even with shorter texts the teacher will need to keep a careful check on the actual reading of the material, ensuring that the students have understood the general outline or framework of the story (see Chapter 4).

2.1.3 *The ability to respond appropriately*

As well as the ability to read fluently there are skills which will contribute to the students' comprehension and enjoyment in a different way. They should, for example, be able to:

- visualise mentally what is described in words
- respond emotionally to the text and identify with, or feel sympathy for, the hero or heroine. This is obviously easier for them if material has been chosen with their interests in mind
- understand the characters' motives
- make critical and moral judgements of varying degrees of sophistication on what they read
- detect the relationship which exists between author and text i.e. be aware of a writer's attitude and purpose and know whether a passage is intended to be taken seriously or not.

Sample Texts for Beginners in Literature

Type of text	Example	Author
Poetry Anthologies	Seven Themes in Modern Verse	M Wollman
	Touchstones Vols 1, 2, 3	M G Benton & P Benton
	Reading and writing poems with students of English	A Maley, S Moulding
Individual Poets	Collected Works	Robert Frost
	Collected Works	James Berry
Short Stories	*Out of Africa*	Karen Blixen
	* *Zero Hour*	Michael Swan (ed.)
	* *Outstanding Short Stories*	Longman Simplified
Plays	*Kongi's Harvest*	Wole Soyinka
	* *An Inspector Calls*	J B Priestley
	* *Arms and the Man*	G B Shaw
Science Fiction	*The Wall Around the World*	S Morris (ed.)
	The Day of the Triffids	J Wyndham
Adventure	* *The Seventh Raven*	Peter Dickinson
	Zed	Rosemary Harris
Human Interest	*Flowers for Mrs Harris*	P Gallico
	Walkabout	James Vance Marshall
	The Pearl	John Steinbeck
Literature	*The Great Gatsby*	Scott Fitzgerald
	* *Animal Farm*	George Orwell
Autobiography	*My Family and Other Animals*	G Durrell

Local Authors

Africa	*Indian Sub-continent*	*Caribbean*
Buchi Emecheta	R K Narayan	V S Naipaul
Chinua Achebe	R Jabvala Prawer	E Braithwaite
Ngugi wa Thiongo	Bapsi Sidhwa	V Reid

* *Cambridge First Certificate set texts*

Figure 2

Can you extend these lists?

2.2 Linguistic and stylistic level

2.2.1 *Linguistic level*

If students have to struggle with extremely difficult vocabulary and sentence structure they will neither understand the text nor enjoy reading it. Texts should therefore be chosen with the following points in mind:

- vocabulary and text structure within the students' scope
- slang, dialect and highly idiomatic language at a minimum.

Vocabulary and text structure

(a) Students should be able to infer the meaning of most of the unknown words from the context. Ideally these should not occur more frequently than one or two in every hundred (Bright and McGregor 1970). Complex sentence structure also makes it difficult for students to infer the meaning of unknown words.

(b) Vocabulary should not, in general, be:

- dated e.g. 'I say, how *jolly awful*, Jeeves,' I said
- archaic e.g. *quoth* he, I *fain* would see it
- overspecialised or technical e.g. the terms *shillets* and *belving* taken from otter hunting in *Tarka the Otter* by H Williamson.

Students are unlikely to meet such language elsewhere and it has little value for them, especially in the early stages of a course.

(c) It should be possible for students to see how one part of the text relates to another, both at sentence and paragraph level. They should, for example, be able to recognise the signals contained in the lexical and grammatical patterns, including the connectors such as *however*, *thus* and *therefore*. They will then be able to discover the general framework of any passage, see how examples relate to preceding generalities and follow a passage of exposition or argument to its conclusion. Sentence structure must therefore be at a level that they can handle. The dense style of Henry James, for example, would be quite unsuitable for most students below university level.

Task: Study the following sentence from *The Turn of the Screw* by Henry James, where the governess is first being shown around the house by the little girl.

> Young as she was, I was struck, through our little tour, with her confidence and courage, with the way, in empty chambers and dull corridors, on crooked stairways that made me pause, and even on the summit of an old machicolated square tower that made me dizzy, her morning music, her disposition to tell me so many more things than she asked, rang out and led me on.

(a) Underline the main clause. (b) How many subordinate and dependent phrases are there? (c) What does *machicolated* mean?

That sentence contains ten subordinate clauses and dependent phrases to disentangle before one finds the main clause *I was struck with her confidence and courage*. Comprehension is made even more difficult by the obscure lexical item *machicolated* (containing openings in a parapet). Such a text is obviously unsuitable for most EFL/ESL classes.

Slang, idiom and dialect

Slang, idiom and dialect can, of course, be very potent in the creation of atmosphere and background. Slang, however, dates very quickly and both slang and dialect have the disadvantage of:

- calling upon vocabulary and syntax which overseas students are unlikely to meet elsewhere, except perhaps on film or television
- providing false linguistic models.

When slang is used in a token way (e.g. Ralph's *Sucks to your assmar* in *Lord of the Flies*) students can usually cope after some assistance from the teacher. Where it is particularly dense, however, they may either lose interest or get involved in research which will have no great value for them. Idiomatic language is also liable to give students problems in that the meaning of an idiom cannot be deduced from the meanings of its parts. Much of Dickens' work, therefore, which contains a lot of unusual vocabulary and highly idiomatic language (e.g. the slang of Fagin's den in *Oliver Twist*) would be inaccessible to students in the early stages of a literature course. Some indication of ways of dealing with such language at more advanced levels is given in Chapter 5. In ESL classes in Britain modern slang and idiomatic language will not present the barrier to understanding that they do abroad and may even help the students to relate to the text under discussion.

Dialect, like slang, is also difficult for students to cope with due to the high percentage of unknown words and unusual structures. When its use is merely token (e.g. there are snatches of Northern dialect in the short stories of D H Lawrence) students will probably be able to work out the meanings of the individual words.

Task: In this passage from Hardy's *The Mayor of Casterbridge* Abel Whittle, an old countryman, is explaining to Farfrae what had happened to Henchard towards the end.

I seed en go down the street on the night of your worshipful's wedding to the lady at yer side and I thought he looked low and faltering. . .I zeed that he wambled and could hardly drag along.

(a) What do *wambled* and *faltering* mean?

(b) Why has Hardy spelled some words differently (e.g. *seed* and *zeed*)?

While the precise meaning of some of the words may escape us in such a case the conversation is made understandable on the whole by the context and by Farfrae's later comments and reactions.

However, when dialect is presented complete, with different vocabulary, phonetic representation of the spelling and with few clues as to the meaning of individual items then it may be impossible for the student to understand it. The following passage appears, for example, in one of Walter Scott's Waverley novels:

> This day ye have quenched seven smoking hearths—see if the fire in your ain parlour burn the blither for that. Ye have riven the thack of seven cottar houses—look if your ain roof tree stand the faster—Ye may stable your stirks in the shealings at Derncleugh—see that the hare does not crouch on the hearthstand at Ellangowan.

Many native English speakers would have difficulty with that piece of prose and it is best to avoid texts where dialect is so dense. Where, however, slang and dialect figure in a less obvious way (to mark a certain character, for example) the teacher can analyse a few speeches at the beginning so that the students can translate for themselves later on (see Chapter 6).

Assessing linguistic difficulty

Given the problems of lexical and structural difficulty, how can a teacher decide which texts will be 'readable' for a particular class, and which are the ones that the students will be best able to cope with?

Readability formulae The two factors most closely related to the level of difficulty of a given text are: (1) the average number of syllables per word; (2) the average length of the sentence.

Various formulae have therefore been devised to relate these factors to the reading age of native speaker children. Examples of the major formulae, their ease of calculation and so on, can be found in Harrison's *Readability in the Classroom* (1980). Teachers with access to a computer might like to use the Textgrader program (see Appendix).

Although, in practice, the two variables of sentence and word length are a reasonably good guide to the level of difficulty of a text the formulae are not generally designed with the EFL situation in mind. No allowance is made, for example, for the added difficulties of very idiomatic language or culturally biased material. E Fry has devised a readability graph (1977) specifically for use with EFL readers, but it is still based on word and sentence length. Furthermore, since such formulae are usually designed to judge the suitability of texts for native speaker children the results do not always correlate to adult language learners.

Cloze tests   A better method of confirming readability from the teacher's point of view is the cloze test, since it is relatively easy to administer and is directly applicable to the class with whom one wishes to consider the book.

THE CLOZE TEST

The teacher prepares a reasonably typical extract from the novel and deletes words from the passage on a regular basis (usually every sixth or seventh word). The students are then instructed to supply the missing vocabulary. There will need to be at least fifty deletions for the test to have validity and, for this sort of assessment, sensible alternatives should not be marked as correct. Obviously there will be some words (e.g. proper names) which it will be impossible for the students to guess, but in the final analysis such omissions will be unimportant. Average class results should yield the following information:

- more than 57 per cent correct: the text can be read by students working on their own
- between 44 and 57 per cent: the text can be read with assistance from the teacher
- below 44 per cent: the text is too advanced for the students.

Pooled assessment   The assessments of other teachers in the department should also provide a reasonable guide to the appropriateness of certain texts.

2.2.2 *Stylistic level*

The question of style is, in some ways, a vexed one since there is considerable difference of opinion as to what it is and how it should be taught. Jonathan Swift maintained that it was 'proper words in proper places', a nice following of the rules, in fact. Modern theory suggests that an author's style consists rather of the ways in which he manipulates the rules of the language or even diverges from them. In whatever way it is defined, however, teachers need to be aware of the immense grasp of the technicalities of a language which students must possess in order to appreciate a writer's style and discuss it.

Students must know roughly what constitutes the linguistic norm in order to be able to recognise any deviation as a stylistic device. Language which deviates from the norm for stylistic effect is said to be *marked* or *foregrounded* (made to stand out) and Alex Rodger made the pertinent point:

> Without this solid background in the normative uses of English the ESL student of English literature will be unable to perceive literary foregrounding. . .If he does not know what personal or public prayer sound like in speech or look like in print, he will not recognize the prayer-like implications in poems which imitate prayer, or merely contain subtle echoes of prayer or are parodies of prayer. . .And the same goes for a whole mass of non-literary varieties of discourse in English (Rodger 1983).

In other words, certain stylistic notions can really only be appreciated by students who have had sufficient experience of reading material of a more general literary nature and are aware of the different lexical and structural choice open to an author.

Structural choice

One area of structural choice open to an author is that of word order. Unusual word order may, to some extent, be expected in poetry due to the requirements of rhyme or metre, but it can also be used in prose to create a certain effect. In *Things Fall Apart*, a novel renowned for its simplicity of style, Chinua Achebe describes how Unoka, a gentle lazy man who loves music, is taken to the forest when ill and left there to die. He says:

> Such was Unoka's fate; when they carried him away he took with him his flute.

Students must have prior knowledge that the unmarked sentence would have been *He took his flute with him when they carried him away* to appreciate that the inverted word order adds an extra dimension to the sentence and reinforces the reader's surprise that one so gentle as Unoka, whose sole love was his flute, should be treated in this fashion. Word order thus determines not only sense but emphasis and clearly students must have considerable experience of standard word order for them to see the deviance as a stylistic effect. (See Chapters 6 and 7 for ways of assisting students to develop a feel for the structure and balance of a sentence.)

Lexical choice

An author chooses words which are appropriate to his or her purpose. If he or she is trying to suggest the thoughts of an ordinary person in a colloquial way, he or she will often use slang. Dickens, on the other hand, frequently achieved his comic effects by using pompous and inflated language to talk about everyday things. The opening paragraph of *Oliver Twist* contains the words 'item of mortality' for 'baby' and says that the surgeon had considerable difficulty in 'inducing Oliver to take upon himself the office of respiration' when he means 'getting him to breathe'.

The author thus takes into account not only the basic meanings of words but also their connotations, the areas of association that accompany them. Thomas Keneally in his novel *Passenger*, for example, uses many gynaecological terms not in common usage but necessary to the work since he is trying to describe the life of an unborn child, the 'passenger' of the title. Such technical vocabulary can be used to give an appearance of reality to a text and students need to be familiar with the connotations. If they are aware of the choices open to an author they will realise the significance of the words he has chosen.

Prior knowledge is also important in understanding idiomatic language and slang. P G Wodehouse's stylistic device of expanding and extending common idioms is a case in point. In order to understand the meaning of *up to the neck in bouillon*, for example, students must know: (1) the original idiom *in the soup* meaning 'in trouble'; (2) that bouillon is a kind of soup.

It is useless therefore to choose texts of great stylistic complexity for the early stages of a literature syllabus and analysis of style at any level should be based on the linguistic features with which the students are already fully familiar.

2.2.3 *Grading texts*
Texts set in the initial stages of a literature course will be radically different from those set at examination level and some sort of progression is needed. This is often:

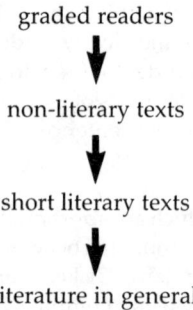

graded readers

↓

non-literary texts

↓

short literary texts

↓

literature in general

The exception is poetry which can be included at any level providing structure and lexis are suitable.

Graded readers Texts of fiction and non-fiction which are either:
- new texts written to strictly controlled language specifications
- existing texts which have been altered or modified in some way to conform to the same specifications as the newly written texts.

Existing texts, including works by famous authors, may be abridged, simplified or totally rewritten (see Hedge 1985:1–20 for a full discussion of methods of simplification). In totally rewritten works minor characters disappear, the story sequence is changed so that it follows chronological order and almost all of the writer's original language is omitted. This frequently leaves a disarticulated skeleton of character and plot which bears only a slight resemblance to the original work.

While reading such texts may solve the problem of linguistic difficulty and provide extensive reading at a level at which the students can cope, it cannot be regarded as literature study. Some abridged versions of famous novels retain enough of the original to preserve some of the 'flavour' of the work and some have stories exciting enough to carry the reader along despite the bareness of the prose. However, if it is going to be possible for the students to read the whole text later then it is generally better for them to do so. Graded readers are, nevertheless, a very useful introduction to extensive reading and should help students improve their reading speed.

Non-literary texts Authentic texts written for native English speakers and not altered in any way to simplify them for the foreign learner.

Reading such texts should enable students to acquire the background information and reading skills necessary for the grasp of 'true' literature later on. Bright and McGregor speak of the 'virtuous circle' whereby the more the student reads 'the more background he acquires of other ways of life and the more he finds he can understand' (Bright and McGregor 1970:52).

Literary texts Initially shorter works such as Orwell's *Animal Farm* or Scott Fitzgerald's *The Great Gatsby*, progressing finally to literature in general.

There will come a time when students are able to cope with set texts in much the same way as a native speaker, but this is not usually before the sixth form in ESL classes in Britain and university level abroad. Up to this point therefore teachers must continue to choose carefully the kinds of texts they include and give considerable assistance with the actual reading (see pages 47-48). Students taking the literature option of the Cambridge Proficency Examination, for example, still need a lot of help with the text itself.

2.3 Background

Foreign students' understanding of a text can also be hampered by their lack of background knowledge of the English or American way of life. The differences they encounter may lead to a degree of 'cultural displacement', but can also make a positive contribution to their enjoyment.

Problem features

Differences in:
- social conventions and customs
- attitude and values
- social class distinctions
- religious or political ideas
- geographical features and climate
- diet and dress
- historical background

Positive features

Enrichment by:
- widening of horizons
- knowledge of other ways of life
- entrance to the world of imagination
- appeal to universal human emotions

Teachers must bear in mind the amount of time they will have available for background explanation when choosing their texts. Even a tale as apparently neutral as Orwell's *Animal Farm*, in that it deals with animals rather than people and is set in the no-man's land of political fable, is, in fact, firmly rooted in the English countryside. Nothing could be more English than Manor Farm; when the pigs finally join the humans they subscribe to *John Bull*, *Titbits* and *The Daily Mirror*, magazines and newspapers noted for their overt patriotism and sensational reporting. The cultural background to that single piece of information could easily take a whole lesson of explanation. If the students are to catch the full flavour of certain texts the background will have to be carefully explained so that they can grasp the underlying as well as the obvious comment.

Furthermore students not only need to have some idea of the differences in historical periods, geographical areas and social classes, but also the topics and themes commonly associated with such divisions. This will enable them to appreciate why certain texts had such an impact in their day. In order to understand the importance of the novel *Room at the Top* or the play *Look Back in Anger*, for example, students must have at least some idea of the social changes occurring in Britain in the fifties and sixties and the kinds of conflict which those changes generated.

There is clearly a case for introducing local authors (including translations into English of the local literature) early on. Local writers tend to deal with situations familiar to the students who do not therefore have to cope with cultural as well as linguistic difficulty. The style of many Commonwealth writers is often simpler than that of English and American authors (although this is not always the case) and such idioms as they use are likely to be better known in their own area than those commonly used by native speakers. This is particularly true where English is a second and not a foreign language. Achebe's *Things Fall Apart*, for example, can provide a successful introduction to literature in English for African students. In the same way *Short Stories from India, Pakistan and Bangladesh* (ed. Ash), an excellent anthology of translated short stories by Tagore, Janeindra Kumar and others, might be equally successful in the Indian sub-continent. Publishers are now releasing not only more individual titles but also a range of guides to Commonwealth literature.

Task: Draw up a list of local titles which you think might be popular in your area. Do not forget the criteria of brevity and simplicity.

In addition to such local literature teachers can also turn to English writers (e.g. Graham Greene, Somerset Maugham) who have written books set in foreign places. These, although representing a European point of view, may contain enough local material to provide reassurance for students just starting literature studies.

Differences of background, whether religious, political or cultural, can be exploited by the teacher and prove a strength rather than a liability. Where there are correspondences between the Western way of life and that of others these can be used to advantage; often comparison of similar problems faced by different cultures is very rewarding.

John Carey, in an article in *The Sunday Times*, described a visit to a university campus in India, a continent currently undergoing an industrial revolution in some areas similar to the one in Britain witnessed by Dickens. Carey wrote:

All along the university perimeter, on the dirt sidewalk, were neat piles of cooking utensils belonging to pavement dwelling families. The grown-ups were off doing casual labour. The toddlers could be seen playing almost naked on muck heaps. Slightly older children were patiently sorting piles of plastic bags, rags and bottles for resale. Krook, the rag and bone dealer in *Bleak House*, would have felt quite at home (Carey 1983).

Teachers should be alert to see the connection between the themes of literature and those of everyday life.

These correspondences, often treated by people from totally different backgrounds, can reveal the universality of human emotions and values. Symbol and metaphor may point up the similarities.

> *Task*: Find the snake episode in the first chapter of Camera Laye's *The Dark Child* and compare it with D H Lawrence's poem *Snake*, where both look upon the snake as a god representing primeval power and innocence.

Care should be taken not to choose books from the same social background each time. As well as books set in middle class society there must also be room for the Northern novels, based in working class families, e.g.:

- *Room at the Top* by John Braine (working class)
- *The Franchise Affair* by Josephine Tey (middle class).

The language used in such books is not only different but revealing, telling the reader indirectly a great deal about the characters portrayed. For example, if Millicent says 'The play was too ghastly, my dear' the students must realise that: (1) *too ghastly* means *extremely bad*; (2) *my dear* can be a casual form of address and is not necessarily an endearment; (3) the type of language places the speaker in a certain social class and historical period.

The teacher should therefore help the students to become familiar with the social distinctions revealed by certain expressions. *The Great Gatsby*, for example, is a very popular reader for overseas students, but they will need to know that Gatsby's expression *Old Sport* was a phrase at one time employed by the upper classes (to whom Gatsby pretends to belong) in order to catch fully its falseness when Gatsby uses it.

2.4 Editions and study guides

Problems of background, or stylistic and linguistic difficulty may be minimised by choosing an edition which gives assistance in those areas. Some editions are specially designed for the overseas reader and contain notes and glossaries as well as literary criticism and commentaries. If such an edition is not available it is common for the teacher to compile and supply a study guide to the work, consisting of:

- a glossary of words and expressions
- a set of summaries or pre-questions which bring out the main flow of events in each chapter
- a biography of the author
- a discussion of local customs and background relevant to the text
- a critical analysis of the work.

Although such guides are undoubtedly helpful to students with little background knowledge of the material they represent a great deal of work for the teacher. Teachers might prefer, instead, to recommend one of the professional study guides put out by publishers (e.g. Longman's *York Notes* series or Macmillan's *Master Works*), or introductions to individual authors (e.g. the *Critical Perspectives* series by Heinemann). The danger with that, however, is that the students read the guide and not the novel.

Glossaries   These have disadvantages as well as advantages. It is possible, for example, that students will be less likely to consult a proper dictionary if instant translation is provided and will not, therefore, get to know the range of the lexis.

On the other hand the first reading should be as comprehensible as possible if the students are really to enjoy the work and so some readers (e.g. *Oxford Progressive English Readers*) have difficult vocabulary and idioms explained at the foot of the page. Reference to a dictionary can follow later if a more intensive study of the passage is undertaken.

2.4.1 *Summaries and pre-questions*
Some study guides include a mini-summary of each chapter to ensure that students have grasped the main lines of the plot. Generally speaking a better method is to set some pre-questions which will stimulate the students into reading the chapter themselves.

When the text is longer and more complex pre-questions can point the students towards the main theme, guide them through distracting sub-plots and draw their attention to points of character which they might otherwise have missed (see Chapter 5: Pre-reading). They will also be of assistance in helping them to prepare short summaries of their own.

2.4.2 *Background*
Opinions vary on how much background material should be made available to students, ranging from a complete course on English history, civilisation and literature, to a simple injunction to read the set book by next Thursday. There are no hard and fast rules, but obviously some explanation will occasionally be necessary, such as social conditions of the time, local customs or historical facts which influence the plot and are assumed to be known (e.g. the British retreat from Dunkirk in World War II in *The Snow Goose* by Paul Gallico).

Study aids in the form of educational videos or audio cassettes can also be used to help students with background. Educational videos dealing with great authors and their works are available and can be used in handy segments to augment work at many levels. One such video is *Charles Dickens and Great Expectations* (Penguin Study Video). It takes the form of a dramatised reading by Dickens to a group of Victorians and his discussion of the work with them. Because filmed episodes from the novel are interspersed to illustrate certain points, students have the opportunity of seeing how people lived and dressed in nineteenth century Britain as well as getting a better understanding of the story. The conversations between Dickens and his audience are designed to reveal: (1) facts about the society of the time (e.g. public execution of criminals); (2) insights into the characters and their motives; (3) Dickens' artistic methods.

And in the filmed sequences from the novel the sight of Miss Havisham, all cadaverous face, manic eyes and cobwebs, will explain more in seconds than hours of teacher talking time.

Audio cassettes are also available, some dealing with author and background in a similar way to the videos, some consisting of readings either of classical works or those by modern authors. Most cassettes are abridged in some way, but there are complete versions of several books put out by Cover to Cover publishers. Poetry recordings can also be obtained and are dealt with more fully in Chapter 8 (see also Appendix). The following are examples of high quality cassettes:

- Author and background: *Dickens and his London*
- Classical works: *Nicholas Nickleby* and *David Copperfield*, read by Roger Rees in Dickens' own adaptation for public reading
- Modern works: John Wyndham's *The Chrysalids* read by Robert Powell
- Complete versions: Jane Austen's *Pride and Prejudice*, Charlotte Bronte's *Jane Eyre*.

Why is it valuable to use such aids? How will experience of different voices and accents assist the students?

The British Council should be able to supply help and, in some cases, material. It should be noted, however, that any aid, whether film or cassette, should take a subservient role to the work it is explaining and not be an end in itself.

2.4.3 *Literary criticism*
The traditional Anglo-Saxon approach has been to discourage critical discussion of a work until the reader is satisfied in his own mind as to his feelings about it. This is not necessarily the case elsewhere; in some areas it is common to include the study of relevant literary criticism from the outset. How will the students know what to look for, it is reasoned, if they are not given a critic's guidance?

Both points of view are valid. It is, however, necessary for the students eventually to develop a feel for the text themselves and to be able to express what *they* think the novel, play or poem is trying to say. Guidance can, of course, be given during the actual reading of the text, but it is important that the students' own ideas be allowed to surface and that their feel for the language being used develops naturally.

> *A Final Point to Consider*: Should these notes, appendices, study guides etc be in English or the mother tongue?

It is generally better for these aids, as with dictionaries, to be in English where students are capable of coping with monolingual reference material. If time is at a premium, however, then notes in the students' own language will speed up comprehension and make discussion possible with greater ease. The teacher will know best which is needed.

A text, therefore, can only possibly have a *literary* value for students if they can both understand the language and relate to the content in a variety of ways. It is also true that where student motivation is high, where the text has a particular interest for them due either to its exciting story or relevance to their way of life, they will be prepared to expend more effort on understanding it; and the problems of cultural displacement and linguistic and stylistic difficulty will become less significant.

For students really to enjoy the material, it is plain that both the teacher's original choice of text and subsequent exploitation of the material are very important.

3 Organising the work

Despite the clear advantages of the use of literature in the classroom from a motivational point of view, its use will not automatically guarantee the students' interest. Teaching should be carefully organised, both at course level and in the presentation of the material, so that students can both enjoy and profit from the work.

3.1 Organising the course

Some teachers will be using literature as part of a general language course, others as part of an examination syllabus, but both have similar final objectives. These are to assist students:
- to understand and enjoy the material as completely as possible (the second being dependent on the first)
- to improve their general command of the language.

In order to achieve those objectives teachers will need to:
1 Draw up a detailed profile of the communicative needs of their students. Are there any particular functions of language, for example, which they will need to practise? Which texts might best exemplify those aspects of language which they will be considering? (E.g. Peter Porter's poem *Your Attention Please* can provide an admirable follow-up to a lesson on formal instruction.)
2 Decide on the amount of time to be devoted to literature specifically. In a general language class one hour a week out of four or five should be devoted to reading and reading related activities, and proportionally the same in an ESP intensive course (i.e. about a quarter of the time).
3 Compile a balanced selection of texts (either whole texts or extracts depending on the time available) including novels, short stories, plays and poems.
4 Find films, cassettes and visual aids of various kinds which will help the students understand the material.
5 Draw up a supplementary reading list for the student who works at a faster pace and for follow up work.

6   Teachers of examination classes should know what type of questions are liable to be asked during the examination and build methods of attack for such questions into the course. (*Passing in Literature* by Hindmarsh (1971) contains many excellent examples of exam questions and methods of approach.)

The 1986 Cambridge First Certificate suggests as optional set texts:
- J B Priestley, *An Inspector Calls*
- George Orwell, *Animal Farm*
- Peter Dickinson, *The Seventh Raven*
(1) Which might you choose to set first to your class?
(2) What graded readers might you consider setting as preparation?

As a general principle works should be covered as quickly as is consonant with the students' understanding and benefiting from the reading.

3.2 Organising work on a set text

Before presenting any text to the students prepare it carefully youself to ensure that the basic material will be fully understood. Such preparation will involve finding the theme, sorting out background problems, drawing up a scheme of work and then planning the individual lessons.

3.2.1 *Finding the theme*
The teacher should always have the main theme of the work clear in mind. Students must understand the theme and how the work deals with it in order to appreciate the material. Most novels or plays involve some sort of conflict and identifying this central opposition is usually one of the quickest ways of getting to grips with a story.

The conflict can take a variety of forms. The hero or heroine may clash with the prevailing standards or moral values of the society in which they live (e.g. Mr Rochester in *Jane Eyre*) and the novel records the outcome of the conflict. They may triumph over exceptional and difficult circumstances or be destroyed by them. The work may contrast the life style of different communities or social groups, or a traditional way of life with a modern life style. One of the themes of *Lord of the Flies*, a text considered at some length in this book, is the contrast between 'civilised' and 'primitive' values.

Ideally one should group studies of texts around a particular theme, such as *heroes and heroines* or *violence and despotism*. Jot down any material which is relevant to the theme and then choose the texts which are accessible to your

Scheme of Work for *Lord of the Flies* by William Golding

Theme: Tyranny and violence

Texts: *Lord of the Flies* by William Golding, Faber 1954. *Hawk Roosting* by Ted Hughes.
Simplified or Abridged versions of *The Coral Island* by R M Ballantyne, *Robinson Crusoe* by Daniel Defoe

Supplementary material: Film *Lord of the Flies*, 1962 directed by Peter Brook

Assumptions: That students have read *Animal Farm* by Orwell and *Of Mice and Men* by J Steinbeck

Aims: To ensure mainly content knowledge

Period	Pre-reading Discussion	Passage	Focus of Discussion	Supplementary Activities	Background Material	Homework Passage and Pre-questions
1	Predictions Title	7–10	Introduction to Ralph, Piggy and the island	Gp work: Priorities when marooned	Short 'life' of Golding	10–19
2	Answering pre-questions (the conch)	19–25	Jack and the choir	Gp work: Types of government	Difference state/public schools	25–38
3	Jack not killing the pig	38–42	The beast: Piggy's character	Review questions Comparison *Robinson Crusoe*		42–60

4	Simon	60–62	Simon	Gap-filling exercise	Epilepsy	62–74
5	Answering pre-questions	74–79	The dispute about the fire	Role-play: First read and act then interview		79–109
6	The airman	109–111	The airman: Sam and Eric	Story-telling game; Planning a film	Parachutes	111–123
7	Predictions	123–127	The imitation pig-killing	Lists of children's games; Hawk Roosting	Pig in the Middle, Tag, Pax	127–140
8	Simon's vs Piggy's response	140–141 147–151	Simon: Killing the pig	Comparison Coral Island and Animal Farm	'Sacred' disease; Beelzebub	151–167
9	Levels of violence	167–170	Simon's death	Group predictions: what should Ralph and Piggy do		170–195
10	Predictions reviewed	195–201	Piggy's death	Gp work: Symbolism (fire, conch, snake, glasses)		201–223
11	Uniforms	220–223	Painted faces	Foreshadowing diagram		
12	EVALUATE—SHOW THE FILM					

Figure 3

students. Many will be too long or too complex for an EFL student in the early stages of a literature syllabus, but it might be possible to read some theme-related material in simplified or abridged versions. When looking at *Lord of the Flies*, for example, related 'shipwreck' stories such as *The Coral Island* by R M Ballantyne or *Robinson Crusoe* by D Defoe could be set as extra reading in their simplified versions so that the students have some means of reference (see the Scheme of Study).

3.2.2 *Sorting out background problems*
Go through the text to be studied in advance and make a list of all the problem areas it will be necessary to deal with, both before and during the reading.

In the case of poetry ask yourself if there is any vocabulary which it is vital for students to know. In a novel, are there any historical or cultural facts crucial to an uderstanding of the story? Is there an educational video or film of the work which could be used with the class? Are there any professional recordings on tape?

List any information about the author's life which would be helpful (e.g. the fact that William Golding went to a private boarding school is relevant to his work *Lord of the Flies*).

3.2.3 *Drawing up a scheme of work*
As it is usually necessary to read more material together than would perhaps be the case in a mother tongue literature lesson, a careful scheme of work needs to be envisaged.

With poetry, short stories and most plays it is often possible to read the entire text in class, but with the novel a slightly different approach is needed.

Choose several fairly lengthy passages to go through with the students, ideally at least one per chapter. These passages should be selected for the way in which they:
- contribute to the development of the main story
- highlight one or more of the characters
- add to the social picture drawn by the novel
- demonstrate distinctive traits of the author's style (at this stage of a fairly basic kind).

Such a scheme of work is shown for *Lord of the Flies* on pages 34-35.

The first passage chosen needs to be quite near the beginning, the first few pages, if at all practicable, and feature one or more of the principal characters.

Take, for example, the first three pages of *Lord of the Flies*. The novel traces what happens to a group of school boys stranded on a desert island in time of war. In the beginning of the story they are bound by the rules of the society which they have just left and behave in a 'civilised' manner. Gradually, however, the lack of restraints tells on their conduct and they degenerate into a bunch of savages who engage in ritual killing. The very first few paragraphs give hints of the conflict to come:

> The boy with fair hair lowered himself down the last few feet of rock and began to pick his way towards the lagoon. Though he had taken off his school sweater and trailed it now from one hand, his grey shirt stuck to him and his hair was plastered to his forehead. All around him the long scar smashed into the jungle was a bath of heat. He was clambering heavily among the creepers and broken trunks when a bird, a vision of red and yellow, flashed upwards with a witch-like cry; and this cry was echoed by another.
>
> 'Hi!' it said, 'wait a minute!'
>
> The undergrowth at the side of the scar was shaken and a multitude of raindrops fell pattering.
>
> 'Wait a minute,' the voice said, 'I got caught up.'
>
> The fair boy stopped and jerked his stockings with an automatic gesture that made the jungle seem for a moment like the Home Counties.

This passage introduces the opposition between the jungle, full of creepers, brightly coloured birds and hints of wildness and the young schoolboy in his grey shirt, pulling up his socks as the conventions of Home Counties' society dictate. Two of the leading characters, Ralph and Piggy, are also introduced, and hints given as to the background of each: Ralph in school uniform leading the way; Piggy, slightly ungrammatical of speech, trailing behind. Even primitive ritual might be suggested by the bird's *witch-like* cry.

Reading the first three pages would thus establish:

- why the boys were stranded on the island
- the sort of characters who will play a leading role in the story: Ralph, the natural athlete and Piggy, the figure of fun
- certain elements of Golding's methods and style.

The students will notice, for example, that they cannot find 'flinked' in the dictionary; that Golding does not tell the reader what Ralph thinks of Piggy initially, but leaves him to infer it from Ralph's actions; that the dialogue often appears incomplete. Reading these pages together, therefore, would form a good introduction to the book and an excellent springboard for further discussion. From there the teacher could move on to the next passage, developing the theme and introducing more characters.

The sections chosen should provide the students with the skeleton or framework of the story, allowing them to see the development of the tale as a whole. They can be seen as stepping stones by which the students can get from the beginning to the end of the story in the teacher's company and one might expect anything from five to fifteen passages to form the basis of discussion, depending upon the complexity of the work. Twelve periods of work, as suggested in the scheme of study on pages 34-35 might represent a term's work on set text. With more advanced students more of the reading can be left for them to accomplish privately.

3.3.4 Planning the individual lessons
Individual lessons will also need to be carefully organised. Usually each lesson should consist of:
- Pre-reading discussion
- The reading
- Supplementary activities and follow up work
- Preparation for the following lesson
- A review of some sort.

Chapter 4 discusses at length how these different factors can be included.

3.3 Organising supplementary activities

While the actual reading of the text and teacher-directed activities will constitute a certain part of the lesson there are a variety of activities in which the class, both as a group and as individuals, can participate. These may include:
- role play of various kinds (both scripted and unscripted)
- games or competitions
- watching a film of the novel or play
- planning a film (choosing locations, actors, actresses, scenes to include etc)
- preparing the story as a newspaper report with appropriate headlines etc
- open discussion of a set theme.

Almost any exercise which can be done individually—such as sets of comprehension questions or gap-filling or sequencing exercises—can also be done in groups and examples of all these activities may be found throughout the book.

Activities of this nature are invaluable to the teacher in that they provide:
- a break in the lesson format

- intensive oral practice for students in a relatively free and creative way, giving them an opportunity to develop their communicative competence
- an opportunity for shyer pupils to express themselves
- a focal point for practising particular language functions
- a stimulus for reading and writing exercises.

If, in a role-play situation, the students have assumed the role of a character from the book they are studying it might also:
- give them a deeper insight into the character's motives and actions
- enable them to see the deeper meaning of the dialogue by having to think through what to say themselves.

Such activities need very careful organisation if they are to be successful. Role-play (including drama) and open discussion of a theme have particular difficulties and are considered below.

3.3.1 *Role-play*

There are two basic types of role-playing:
1 students participate in situations in which they play themselves in their everyday roles but having to react to different stimuli;
2 students are assigned a character (in literature study this could well be a person taken from the story) and are asked to think, talk and react as they imagine the person would.

Introductory work

A good introduction to role-play work is the miming game where the students are each given a simple action to mime in turn (such as discovering that they have lost their purse on the bus) and the others have to guess what it is. From there they can progress to role-play in pairs.

The Bus-stop situation

Student A: Complain to the person next to you that he/she is treading on your toes.

Student B: Somebody accuses you unjustly of treading on his/her toes. Politely point out that it was not you.

Some excellent role-play situations of this sort can be found in Revell's *Teaching Techniques for Communicative English* (1979). Certain drills and exercises can also be practised beforehand to assist students with the language they may need.

The format

There are three areas to consider in setting up a role-play situation:
1 the situation;
2 the roles;

ASSIGNMENT CARD   *Side 1*

The Restaurant Owner
(Role-play based on *The Moon
is Down* by John Steinbeck)

YOUR ROLE
You are the owner of the
Kursaal restaurant, your wife is
the cook and you have a waiter.
YOU HATE THE INVADERS

THE SITUATION
You are discussing the news
brought by Dr Winter that
Mayor Orden is to be executed
when two soldiers enter and
order a meal. (The waiter takes
the order.) You tell your wife to
oversalt the first course and
burn the dessert. Warn your
waiter and tell him to serve the
meal as usual. When they
complain to your waiter go and
apologise to them. Offer them
their money back if it becomes
absolutely necessary.

ASSIGNMENT CARD   *Side 2*

YOUR ATTITUDE
You are very polite to the
soldiers and you apologise, but
they can see you are not really
sorry.

USEFUL PHRASES
About Mayor Orden

Isn't it $\left\{ \begin{array}{l} \text{terrible} \\ \text{disgusting} \\ \text{frightening} \end{array} \right\}$ about

Apology
I'm sorry/very sorry/most upset
I don't know how it happened
It's not always possible to
judge . . .
Perhaps you would prefer . . .
(your money back)
Can I offer you . . . (your money
back)
I'm sure you understand
that . . .

Figure 4

3 the strategies for dealing with the situation.
This information can be given on a set of assignment cards, each of which
(a) identifies the student's role and, possibly, the attitude he or she should
    adopt;
(b) sketches the situation briefly and offers suggestions as to how it should
    develop;
(c) since there is no formal written script, lists any useful information
    which students might need to cope with the situation.
Such strategic information can include:
• vocabulary
• grammatical features appropriate to the speech functions likely to occur
  (e.g. ordering a meal, complaining, etc)
• socio-linguistic features (e.g. degrees of formality etc)
• perhaps a sample dialogue.

Sample situation

The following is a situation based on *The Moon is Down* by John Steinbeck, about a small town invaded and occupied by the Germans during World War II.

Situation: A restaurant owner and his wife/cook are discussing the news brought by Dr Winter that Mayor Orden is to be executed. Two soldiers enter the restaurant and order a meal. The owner instructs his wife to put too much salt in the first course and burn the dessert. The soldiers at first complain and then threaten. The owner is very apologetic and offers them their money back. They leave.

Roles (5): The restaurant owner, his wife, a waitress/waiter, two soldiers.

Strategies: Language needed for ordering, apologising, complaining etc.

Items needed: A menu for the soldiers to order from.

Follow-up work: Students to write the story as the restaurant owner would tell it to Dr Winter.

Figure 4 on page 40 shows an assignment card for the restaurant owner.

As a general principle, any direct intervention by the teacher should be kept to a minimum since the aim is for the students to communicate in a relatively free and creative way. Teachers, could, however, cast themselves in one of the roles if they thought there might be a problem and assist in that way. The diagram below shows how role-play can be set up and then exploited.

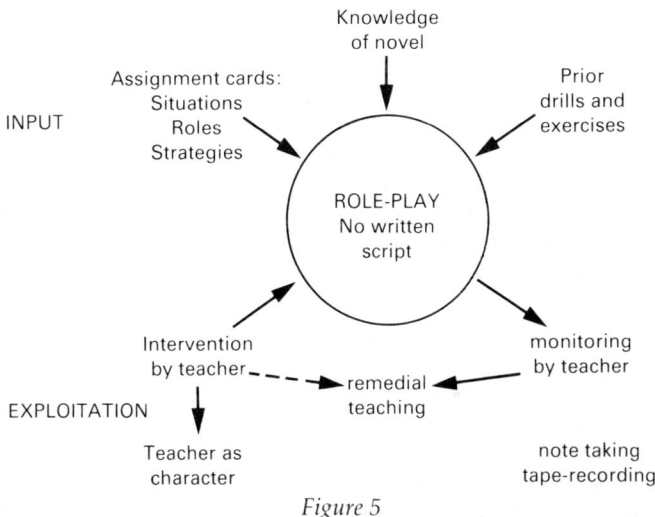

Figure 5

Drama

The major difference between role-play and the acting of a play is that with a play the script is provided, and often in language that is considerably beyond the improvisational abilities of the students. This does not mean that it is not a good idea to have the students act it out. This is always preferable to their reading it from their desks since it means that:

- they can both see and hear the character speak and can thus identify him in a concrete way
- they can envisage the dialogue as a series of meaningful personal exchanges.

It is also a good idea to let them see or hear the entire version on film or recording (see Appendix) since this will help them to make as much sense as possible of the play to begin with.

When the cast is first decided upon equip each student with some property oddment which will identify them (e.g. a pen and notebook for Inspector Goole in *An Inspector Calls* by J B Priestley, or a sceptre-like object for Danlola, the deposed king, in Soyinka's *Kongi's Harvest*). The class will then have an easier job of keeping track of who is who. As many as possible should be assigned some role, no matter how small. Even a linguistically weak student can be stage manager and look after the props.

As with role-play it is better not to interrupt too much (e.g. to correct pronunciation) while the reading is taking place, since it is imperative not to halt the flow of the dialogue. Students can generally understand the rapid exchanges between one speaker and another. As it is the long speeches which often lose them, these can be considered separately later on. Sometimes it will be sufficient to get them to give the teacher the gist of the speech with the teacher reading through again anything which is unclear.

If the school has a theatre, it will help the students to envisage the play if certain sections of it are acted in the theatre. Preparatory work such as the meanings of certain terms (upstage, downstage, right and left of stage and so on) should be done first in the classroom. Students are sometimes shy in such a setting, but soon adapt to the greater amount of space and learn to project themselves. (Another book in this series will deal with Drama fully.)

3.3.2 *Discussion*

Free discussion of a set theme or subject raised in the novel, poem or play is the most obvious choice for group activities and one of the most difficult to organise satisfactorily. Subjects are not difficult to find. A number of different aspects can form the basis for discussion:

- *Character:* Is Captain MacWhirr really stupid? (*Typhoon* by Conrad)

- *Themes:* Is it possible for all men to be equal? (*Animal Farm* by George Orwell)
- *Moral questions:* Should Jane have stayed with Rochester despite his mad wife? (*Jane Eyre* by Charlotte Bronte)

However, there is really no such thing as 'free' discussion of a theme. The scene must be set clearly, sufficient guidance given and material provided or the project will fail. The groups will be sitting around saying nothing or, if a monolingual class, carrying on a conversation in their own language.

It is no good sending students away to discuss 'Symbolism in the *Lord of the Flies*'. The point is too general and once they have decided that the conch is symbolic a deep silence will fall. Nor should yes/no questions be set since once the 'correct' alternative has been chosen the subject is closed. Teachers soon discover that they must not only carefully define the areas of discussion, but also supply most of the argument.

As with role-play assignment cards are the best answer. They can contain:
- a list of questions or statements with which students can agree or disagree
- references to page numbers where answers and ideas may be found
- strategies for conducting the discussion.

A secretary to the group should be appointed with instructions to record their answers to the questions or reactions to the statements. Occasionally a truly difficult question can be included to make the group search hard to find the answer. By doing so it is hoped they will acquire the skill of retrieving specific facts from the text.

Examples of the types of question which can be set and the way subjects can be distributed can be found in Chapters 4 and 6. Once the groups are quite happy about their own subject for discussion they can come together as a class and compare notes. They should see the way in which their theme has been used overall in the book and ties in with the themes assigned to other groups.

Problems

There are several dangers attached to such group activities of which the most obvious are:
- the increased noise factor
- the problem of keeping track of what each group is up to.

There are no perfect solutions, but the following suggestions may assist:
1 Place a maturer member of the class in each group.
2 Have answers, reactions, comments etc recorded by a group secretary— they will have to produce something at the end.

3 Where it is possible somehow to mark the results so that groups are in competition, point out that marks will be taken off for speaking in any language other than English. The groups will then keep a check on each other over this point at least.

Another of the dangers, perhaps the greatest one, is that insufficient time will be allowed for the discussion. Although it is perfectly possible to have short 'buzz' groups for five or ten minutes at the beginning or end of a session, usually time should be allotted not only for the discussion but also for its exploitation. Time is needed to analyse with them what came out of the discussion. The secretaries can report back. Are all the groups agreed about points of character, twists of the plot? Teachers are often surprised at what has not been grasped completely and how this missed clue has distorted the students' ideas about the novel or play as a whole.

In order to exploit the group session to the full it can help to tape record one of the groups, although it is better not to try and play it back straight away. Half of it will be inaudible for one reason or another—external noise, chatter from other groups, indistinct speech and so on—and nothing will be achieved. Go through it yourself alone first and find out what aspects of the text have not been grasped, what language has not been used. Then in the following lesson, review in a general way such faults and omissions as you think important to correct. If someone made a particularly valid point during the course of the discussion and the recording is clear play that to them.

In conclusion it must be said that one of the most important aspects of group work and supplementary activities of this kind is that they do not appear to be a pointless exercise. All too often group work is looked upon by the students as an easy option; they feel that its main aim is to give the teacher a rest. The session must be shown to have specific language aims and purpose within the general scheme of study for the text as a whole. Then it will be both interesting and rewarding and the students' pleasure in participating will be heightened.

4 Approach to text—Content

The study and critical appraisal of a literary text is an endeavour to come to as full an understanding of the work as possible. The teacher must first help the students enjoy what they read, however, before they can proceed to any sort of effective analysis of the text. This is something that EFL teachers often find hard to do, particularly when the text is a novel, since it is sometimes the sheer volume of material that daunts both student and teacher alike. How should they start to analyse the text? At which end, so to speak, should they begin?

4.1 Content versus form

Initially the teacher must decide just what aspects he or she is trying to draw to the students' attention. Will it be mainly:
content—basically what the play, novel or poem is all about
or will it be:
form—how it is written rather than what is written.
Form and content are inextricably linked, one dependent on the other, but in practice it is possible to stress one particular aspect.

All too often in the past, unfortunately, the teacher's contribution to any discussion of a text under consideration consisted of a form of criticism relating to the literary worth of the passage. It was assumed that the students had understood the material and that the teacher could therefore get on with what literature was all about: the themes, the imagery and symbolism, the structure and the author's technique.

However, what is really needed in the early stages of a literature syllabus is help with the material itself. Time should be spent on the content, ensuring that the students have grasped the main point of the poem, or the bare bones of the plot; that they are familiar with the vocabulary; that they understand the characters. The type of novel chosen at this stage is liable to be a 'realistic' one and the teacher can concentrate on the story, judging, perhaps, how straight a transcript from life the text may be, how willingly one suspends disbelief, in what ways the characters are 'real' people.

Lord of the Flies will again be used for illustration purposes.

4.2 Presenting the material

4.2.1 *Pre-reading discussion*

In order to introduce the material chosen it is sometimes sufficient just to read through the section together. The opening pages of *Lord of the Flies*, for example, are quite exciting and thought-provoking in themselves. Usually, though, the teacher will want to introduce each section by some activity or discussion which:

- arouses the students' interest in the subject
- focuses any prior knowledge they have of the situation and relates it to the material
- elicits some vocabulary they will need.

When reading a passage relating to the violence on the island, for example, the teacher can start off by raising the question of violence generally and sound out the students' theories on the subject e.g.:

- Why does violence occur?
- What provokes or encourages it?
- What is the most effective means of controlling it?

The students, working in pairs or groups, can make lists of any violent situations known to them or the teacher can read a local newspaper report on an incident of violence and discuss it with them.

Another way of introducing material is to have the students make predictions about what is to come.

Predictions

The use of the prediction method has the advantage of calling on the students' knowledge of the plot in order for them to foresee what is liable to happen in the future. It should therefore concretise their knowledge of what has occurred in the story so far as well as stimulating their interest in what is to come.

Their predictions can be prompted by questions from the teacher. Having read for homework to page 167, for example, where Simon goes up into the mountain, they might then be asked:

- Where has Simon gone?
- What will he find?
- What will the rest do when they realise that there is no beast?

Later, when they have read the following passage and discovered what really did happen to Simon they will be able to relate their predictions to the events of the book and work out how much more likely or unlikely they were.

Pre-questions

Leading questions can also be set with the homework at the previous lesson. Suppose, for example, that the next passage for discussion is that in which Jack and the choir appear for the first time.

Set the students pages 10–19 to read for homework and at the same time give them the following questions:

- What sort of life did Ralph and Piggy have before coming to the island?
- What did they find in the lagoon and how did they use it?
- Were there many other people on the island?
- Who were Sam and Eric?

At the beginning of the next lesson someone should be able to answer those questions, providing information vital to an understanding of the situation developing on the island and introducing the all important symbol of the conch. The way has thus been prepared for the arrival of Jack, also a natural leader and a threat to Ralph's authority.

It is not only the teacher who can ask questions. Students can also prepare questions on the passage they have read for homework and can ask them at the beginning of the next lesson. The amount of reviewing and reflection required for them to formulate sensible questions for their classmates is a valuable end in itself.

Pre-reading discussion is therefore very important but should in general be short, relative to the length of the lesson as a whole (cf Williams 1984:37–45 for further examples of Pre-reading Activities).

4.2.2 *Read through the passage*

Although class readings have to be carefully managed they do have value because:

- they ensure that at least some of the reading is accomplished
- the students will all be at the same spot at the same time and able to share the same experiences and profit from any discussion
- where there are puzzling allusions, implications or overtones of meaning it is advantageous to have the words read aloud; correct stress will sometimes explain more than ten minutes of teacher talking time
- certain kinds of text, such as drama and poetry, are obviously designed to be read aloud and are not so effective if this is not done.

Class reading does not mean that the students themselves will always read the material. Many of us can remember those dreary 'reading round' exercises when we were at school, with the slowest member of the class stumbling painfully through lengthy paragraphs while the entire, overall picture of the work was lost. Rather, in order to ensure that the brighter half do not 'turn off' until their turn comes round again, the passage needs to be broken down into sections and a variety of different methods used actually to accomplish the reading.

PROCEDURES FOR READING IN CLASS

- The teacher reads the whole passage. This may well be necessary if the passage is particularly complex or contains a fairly high proportion of unknown vocabulary.
- The teacher reads the narrative and selected students read the dialogue. Where this method is employed it is best to retain one student for the same role each time.
- Selected pupils read sections.
- Students read in groups. This can either be section by section or narrative and dialogue.
- Students read silently. They can be given small tasks to accomplish during the reading, e.g. finding certain vocabulary or the answers to some questions.
- The teacher plays a cassette recording of the extract.
- Students prepare a role-play activity based on the passage.
- A combination of any or all of the above.

4.2.3 *Keep to a programme*

It is necessary to keep to a programme and ensure that the students cover the assigned material in their own time. The teacher can stipulate how many pages are to be covered before the next class and set them pre-questions to motivate them to accomplish that. It should be possible to check how they are keeping up with the reading by the story telling game.

THE STORY TELLING GAME

In this exercise the teacher points at a student who starts to tell the story but who must stop when the teacher's finger points somewhere else. It is more useful and more of a game if the finger moves unpredictably and rests for quite widely differing intervals. Any suggestion of a test is obviously self-defeating in terms of student enjoyment. In order to prevent people speeding through the last hundred pages in a sentence or two a system can be introduced whereby, if a valid point is missed, the person signalling it takes up the story.

Although this might seem a somewhat juvenile exercise adult students also derive a lot of satisfaction from it.

Prediction is also a good means of ensuring continued interest. It can take the form of having students decide on likely sequels to what they have just read or forecasting how the story will finish.

4.2.4 Review regularly

As the readings progress the general framework of the novel should begin to emerge and the way in which the passages chosen relate to the story as a whole should be seen. After each chapter (or a longer section if the teacher judges it appropriate) review questions can be set which can be used to draw out and explain certain allusions, oblique explanations or overtones which the students might have missed on the first reading. Such questions should be designed to get the students to think again about what they have just read. They can either be straightforward comprehension questions or a simple list of items to be ticked true or false.

Here are some sample comprehension questions from Chapter 1 of *The Lord of the Flies*.

(a) How do we know from pages 8 and 14 that a war was going on?
(b) Which words on page 10 show us that Ralph was not interested initially in Piggy's friendship?
   (This should cause them to think about Piggy's character as well as Ralph's).
(c) Why is Ralph so pleased with the island? What sort of climate did he come from?
   (This should cause them to consider how different the children's lives have now become with the change in climate and general environment, the lack of adult supervision, the loss of the rigid caste system of the English public school.)
(d) Why did the boys vote for Ralph as chief?
   (This question will draw their attention to the conch.)

   'But there was a stillness about Ralph as he sat that marked him out: there was his size and attractive appearance; and most obscurely, yet most powerfully, there was the conch. The being that had blown that, had sat waiting for them on the platform with the delicate thing balanced on his knees was set apart.'
(e) Does it matter that there are no adults on the island?
(f) Why didn't Jack kill the piglet?
   (These last two questions will introduce them to one of the main themes of the novel: that without society's restraints people revert to primitive, violent behaviour.)

The virtue of such questions, and they can be considered individually or in groups, is that they compel the students to think again about the story and usually to find in it more than they did before.

The concentrated technique used with Intensive Reading of setting twenty questions on one short paragraph with each item of vocabulary and quirk of syntax examined at length should be avoided, unless the passage is being specifically considered for style. Such an approach will fragment the students' overall vision of the story and probably spoil their enjoyment of the book. The scope of Extensive Reading is broader and speed is more important than depth. The questions can even be set out as a simple true or false exercise, with just a tick to indicate the answer.

Following is a sample True or False exercise:

	True	False
(A) The children had been evacuated to the island because of a war.		
(B) Ralph was not interested in Piggy.		
(C) Ralph did not like the island.		
(D) The boys voted for Ralph as chief because he was the oldest.		
(E) There are no adults on the island.		
(F) Jack did not kill the piglet because he was scared.		

An overview of the contents as a whole is what is desired at this stage; in-depth study can follow later (McGregor 1971:55–57). Because such generally faster reading will encourage the student to deduce the meaning of a word from its context rather than looking it up, this is a far more valuable exercise. More may be lost through failure to establish the sense of the sentence or paragraph as a whole than through ignorance of the meaning of an isolated word. Encourage the students, therefore, to keep their eyes on the context of any unknown vocabulary or puzzling construction; they can explore the exact meaning at a later date if necessary.

Once again the questions can be answered individually or as groups, depending on the amount of time available and the degree of evaluation required by the exercise.

4.3 Introducing further activities and follow-up work

As has been suggested in Chapter 3, it is a good idea to vary the lesson format with as many different activities as possible. Several have been suggested in the Scheme of Work.

4.3.1 *Role-play and improvisation* (Lesson 5)

Not only can certain sections of the book where dialogue is virtually complete be acted out, but scenes not contained in the text can be improvised on the basis of known facts.

The passage in Chapter 4 of *Lord of the Flies*, for example, where Jack and Ralph fall out over Jack's failure to keep the fire going, would be easy to adapt since a lot of the dialogue is given in the text. It should be set out properly in playlet form with the speakers and their actions plainly marked:

Sample situation

Jack: (*excitedly, holding his spear above his head*) Look! We've killed a pig—we stole up on them—we got in a circle.
          (*The hunters all talk excitedly at once.*)

Eric: We crept up—

Sam: We got in a circle—

Roger: The pig squealed.
          (*silence as they all look at Ralph*)

Ralph: You let the fire go out.

Jack: (*still happy and waving his spear*) We can light the fire again.
          You should have been with us Ralph. We had a smashing time. . .

Students can undertake the task of marking up the text as they get a firmer grasp of how the various conventions of speech are applied in the novel.

Later on, when students are comfortable in their roles, it should be possible for them to improvise dialogue which does not occur in the text. The material becomes a focus for their own efforts at communication. Television and radio interviews can be conducted, for example, with the teacher as interviewer and the students as the characters being asked about the events or for their opinions.

Some of the little boys could be asked what they like or do not like about the island (the lack of adults, the physical advantages of the island, their fears about the beast at night). Maurice could be interviewed after the dispute over the fire. The questions can move gradually from the *factual*:

- Who first noticed that the fire had gone out?
- How did Piggy's spectacles get broken?

to the more *evaluative*:

- Do you think Jack was right to hunt for meat instead of keeping the fire going?
- Do you still think Ralph should be leader?
- Why do you think Piggy is the cause of so much friction?

Where necessary the students can be given their questions and a few moments to prepare their replies.

Acting out the roles of the characters helps students gain a deeper insight into events and people's motives and can be integrated into the communicative language teaching programme. Similar interview strategies are used in the Cambridge First and Proficiency examinations.

4.3.2 *Making comparisons* (Lesson 8)

As the class progresses through the story it will be possible to compare characters and themes from other books. The notion of leadership and tyranny also appears in *Animal Farm* and the teacher and students can discuss the use of terror and scapegoats in building the cult image of a leader.

Called upon to find parallels between the two books they should have little difficulty in comparing Napoleon and his savage dogs to Jack and his hunters. It should become obvious that mindless and ritual chanting—*Four legs good, two legs bad* and *Kill the beast! Cut his throat! Spill his blood!*—is a factor in the subordination of rational beings to the will of a tyrant. Distinctive dress and uniforms also play a role.

The students could be given the table on page 53 and told to fill in the missing items.

More or less of the table can be supplied by the teacher and perhaps space could be left for them to add their own parallels.

It might also be possible to judge how *Lord of the Flies* compares with other novels of the 'shipwreck' genre. Students can list, for example, Crusoe's priorities when he landed on the island with those of the children. They can decide if Crusoe managed to fulfil his aspirations. It should also be possible to make the point that previous descriptions of people who have been abandoned or marooned have assumed that the characters preserved intact the traditional moral values from which they have come, even if they are obliged to accept some physical changes in their way of life.

William Golding has overtly compared *Lord of the Flies* to *The Coral Island* and it should be possible to draw up a table, similar to that one shown above, for that book comparing character and moral attitudes.

	Animal Farm	Lord of the Flies
The tyrant	Napoleon	
His henchman		Roger
His army	The dogs	
Rational members of the group		Ralph, Piggy
Mindless chanting		
The tyrant is rarely seen		Jack paints his face
People are punished unjustly		
A scapegoat	Snowball	
Uniforms		
Democratic government abolished		
The efforts of willing workers not rewarded		

Table 1

4.3.3 Discussing different aspects of the work (Lesson 10)

Encourage students to discuss amongst themselves different aspects of the text. Golding's use of symbolism, for example, is one of his most outstanding achievements in the book and a discussion can be set up in the following way.

Sample Group discussion on Symbolism in Lord of the Flies

1 Divide the class into four or five groups (with four or five being the optimum number for each group).
2 Give each group a different item used symbolically in the text (e.g. The Snakes, the Pig's Skull, Piggy's Glasses, The Conch, Fire).

3 Give each group an assignment card containing a list of questions. The assignment card for 'The Conch', for example, contains:

Who find the conch?

Who first uses it?

What is said about the conch's fragility and is this significant?

What did it represent?

Was it a good or bad thing?

What happened when Jack refused to obey it?

What happened when it was broken?

Are there any other items in the book used symbolically?

(References and strategies for discussion can also be provided if necessary.)

4 Once the students have established the answers to their own questions they can come together as a class to see how the symbols used throughout the book point to the theme, the breakdown of civilised values.

4.3.4 *Planning a film of the work* (Lesson 6)

Students can discuss in their groups which scenes they would wish to include, which actors and actresses to star in their production. (They might, for example, like to choose students known to them for the roles.) They can choose suitable music for the various scenes and appropriate locations. They can produce posters advertising the film, hold interviews for the parts and so on. The extent of the involvement is dictated by the amount of time available and the particular communicative functions which the teacher wishes to practise.

4.3.5 *Using visual aids*

Improvised in the classroom

In order to change the focus of attention the teacher can use a variety of visual aids, some of which can easily be improvised in the classroom. They might be:

- a diagram
- a table, as in Table 1
- a map
- a collage or display
- a flow-chart of events or character development.

A map of the island, for example, would obviously help students to place and understand events in *Lord of the Flies*. Sunday magazines often contain interviews with famous authors or a series of photographs inspired by some literary event. *The Sunday Times Magazine* ran a series of photographs on Dickens' London and these could form a set, properly mounted, that the teacher could exhibit in the classroom while any of the Victorian novels was being considered.

Students might contribute to a collage—a long background perhaps onto which they could place pictures and drawings of characters and events, poems, comments etc. These items could be arranged chronologically. Or there could be a map with the items placed according to where the events occurred.

A flow chart can reveal the design or structure of a novel. *Lord of the Flies* is carefully structured to reveal the escalating scale of violence on the island. This is accomplished by a variety of 'foreshadowing' devices whereby initially harmless actions are repeated throughout the book and become more and more violent. This is easy to represent in a flow chart.

THE KILLING GAME

Fun and Games ↓	they play at attacking one another 'a happy, heaving pile' p.29	*Ritual Play*
Mock Violence ↓	Maurice pretends to be the pig p.81	
Half Violence ↓	Robert is forced to be the pig p.126	
Real Violence	Simon is treated as the beast and killed p.168	*Ritual Murder*

A similar chart can be used to show character development (see Chapter 5).

Films and professional recordings (Lesson 12)
Many great works of literature are available in the film or sound version (see Appendix) and they can add greatly to the pupils' appreciation of the material. Seeing the work in a different medium can offer insights into the text which are denied the reader.

In the 1962 film version of *Lord of the Flies*, directed by Peter Brook, there is a marvellous scene near the beginning when Jack and his choirboys join the group for the first time. They come marching along the beach in military formation, dressed in their choir uniforms, while the soundtrack plays a version of *Kyrie Eleison*, Lord have Mercy. The beauty of the music both points up well the 'civilised' life and Christian ethics which the boys have left behind and contrasts greatly with the savagery which is to come. As such it gives the viewer clues which the reader or the book does not receive.

There are a variety of educational video and audio cassettes available and British Council libraries often have films of other materials for hire.

4.3.6 *Evaluating the work* (Lesson 12)

Finally the teacher will want to evaluate the work as a whole. Students should now be familiar with the content and the main themes and the teacher can move on to analyse:

- the author's view of the society he presents
- his attitudes and values.

A teacher could encourage students to consider:

1 Is the children's descent into savagery inevitable?
2 Is it, in fact, desirable and necessary to their survival as a group?
3 Is Golding taking an unduly pessimistic view of human nature?
   These and other questions can be considered in groups and a consensus reached.

And only after as much as possible has been elicited from the students themselves in response to the text would the views of any literary critics be introduced.

5 Approach to text—Character

The consideration of the characters of a novel or play as 'real' people has traditionally been one of the ways of approaching the text. In the initial stages of a literature syllabus this frequently consists of a simple description of physical appearance and personality traits and an account of the ways in which the character is linked with the events of the story.

However, as the students' grasp of the language strengthens and texts considered become more complex, they are able to reach a deeper understanding of the motives and psychology of the characters and can analyse the relationship between themes and structure and the way in which characters are presented. A study of the many varieties and registers of English can also help them to understand the subtle nuances of speech and what these may reveal about the persons in the story. Initially, however, they will start with simple description and can collate the information in a variety of ways.

5.1 Collecting information

Students can begin by making a list of all the major characters involved in the story and collecting all the information they can about each character; they should note page numbers where such information can be found. A dramatis personae is often provided at the beginning of a play and there is usually a physical description of the person given on his or her first appearance on stage.

It is helpful in the early stages if the characterisation is straightforward, as this enables the students to build up a composite picture of the character and form an opinion with relative ease. Characters are often straightforward in this sense in the 'non-literary' books and plays recommended at the start of the study and this should be of assistance to the students.

One such book is *Flowers for Mrs Harris* by Paul Gallico, about a London charlady's trip to Paris to buy herself a Dior dress. The central character, Mrs Harris, is simply but strongly drawn. She is described on the first page of the book as a small woman with apple red cheeks, greying hair and *shrewd, almost naughty little eyes*. Then, on page 10, we find *saucy* eyes, page 11, *clever, roguish* eyes; page 56, *small, vivid blue* eyes, and then, successively, *alert little* eyes, *small blue eyes glittering like aquamarines*, *sharp knowing* eyes, *bright as button* eyes and finally, the *cheeky regard* of Ada 'Arris coming through the customs with her Dior dress.

From this selection of quotations alone the students would get a very good idea of the little charlady's character and could find the references to Mrs Harris's eyes themselves if told to.

As the students progress they can fill in fuller and fuller descriptions of the characters studied. This can be done under a variety of headings such as:

- physical characteristics and (where important) manner of dress
- the character's situation in society
- personality traits
- relationships with others.

Some of these can be listed on a grid so that information about each person is easily to hand.

In *Typhoon* by Joseph Conrad, for example, a short story about a ship caught in a typhoon in the China seas, the character of the Captain, an older, very phlegmatic man, is contrasted strongly with that of his young and excitable first mate, Jukes. It is revealing for the students to see the two sets of characteristics side by side. They can be laid out in a table as in Figure 6.

Name & Situation	Physical Characteristics		Personality Traits		Relationships With Others	
		page		page		page
MacWhirr	Short	3	Shy	3	A well-liked	
Captain	Stocky	3	Calm & unruffled	4	captain	4
Married	Round shouldered	3	Unimaginative	4	Respected by Rout,	
	Fine gold hair	3	Modest	4	the chief	
	Blue eyes	3	Reliable	7	engineer	9
			A man of few		Liked by Mr Sigg	7
			words	15	Disliked by Sigg's	
			Simple	80	nephew	7
			A just man	84	Doesn't like	
					swearing	21
					Irritates and	
					amuses Jukes	15

Name & Situation	Physical Characteristics	Personality Traits		Relationships With Others	
			page		page
Jukes First mate Unmarried	Young Taller than MacWhirr	Respectful	3	Looks on Rout as a fatherly friend	15
		Friendly & well-meaning	14, 15	Dislikes the second mate	24
		Racist	11, 12	Disrespectful to & contemptuous of	
		Nationalistic	9	the Chinamen	11, 12
		Impetuous	83	Likes his shipmates	14
		Talkative	15		
		Conceited	15		

Figure 6

In order to reinforce the information thus gathered the teacher can play the game *Name That Character* later with the students.

NAME THAT CHARACTER

1 Two students are chosen to play.
2 The other students choose a character from the book or play and list the person's characteristics, starting with the most common traits and ending with any they think most likely to give the game away. Lists of between seven and ten items will be needed e.g.

The Second Mate	Boatswain	Rout	Harry
oldish	small	tall	young
short	short-legged	scant-haired	bullet-headed
shabby	ill-favoured	pale	feared
bad teeth	good-natured	long-armed	arms like a
red-nosed	gruff	sallow face	black-smith
beardless	very strong	bony wrists	insolent face
short-spoken	talkative	a dry stick	swears a lot
a mean little	long-armed	stooping	second engineer
beast	hairy chest	fatherly	
cowardly	resembles an	scholarly hands	
	elderly ape		

3 Both players try to guess the name of the character as the characteristics are read aloud slowly, one at a time. They must signal their desire to answer if they think they know who the person is.

Scoring
Each student is given ten points to start with. A point is deducted on every occasion when a character is wrongly named. Five points are given to the student who names the correct person. The student who collects the most points wins.

Individual sections can then be expanded later in fuller notes with appropriate quotations where personality or attitude is clearly brought out by an event or remark. Under *Relationships With Others*, for example, the students might note the following quotations with respect to Captain MacWhirr's relationship with Solomon Rout, his chief engineer.

5.1.2 Relations with Rout

1 Rout knew too well the value of a good billet. (p.9 & p.79)
2 'For my part', Solomon was reported by his wife to have said once, 'give me the dullest ass for a skipper before a rogue. There is a way to take a fool; but a rogue is smart and slippery.' (p.14)
3 'Keep on hammering. . .builders. . .good men. . .And chance it. . .engines. . .Rout. . .good man.' (p.40)
4 Solomon says. . .That captain of the ship he is in—a rather simple man,. . .has done something rather clever. (p.79)

The ways in which various characters are related to each other, whether by marriage, friendship, enmity or respect can also be represented in diagram form, especially where the novel has a large cast and relations are particularly complex. Figure 7 on page 61 shows such a diagram for *Great Expectations*.

As can be seen from the above set of quotations taken from *Typhoon* character may also be revealed by
• what the person says
• what others say about them.

Obtain a copy of *Typhoon* and find out what made Captain MacWhirr make the following remarks. What does each reveal?
(a) You're always meeting trouble half way, Mr Jukes.
(b) There's nothing amiss with that flag. . .I looked it up in the book. Length twice the breadth and the elephant exactly in the middle.
(c) As long as it's done. . .Had to do what's fair.
(d) I had to give him a push.
(e) There's no room for Captain Wilson's storm strategy here.
(f) If I didn't know you, Jukes, I would think you were in liquor.

Such questions can be set to the class working in groups, with a different character assigned to each group and time allowed for reporting back at the end of the lesson.

Character diagram for *Great Expectations*

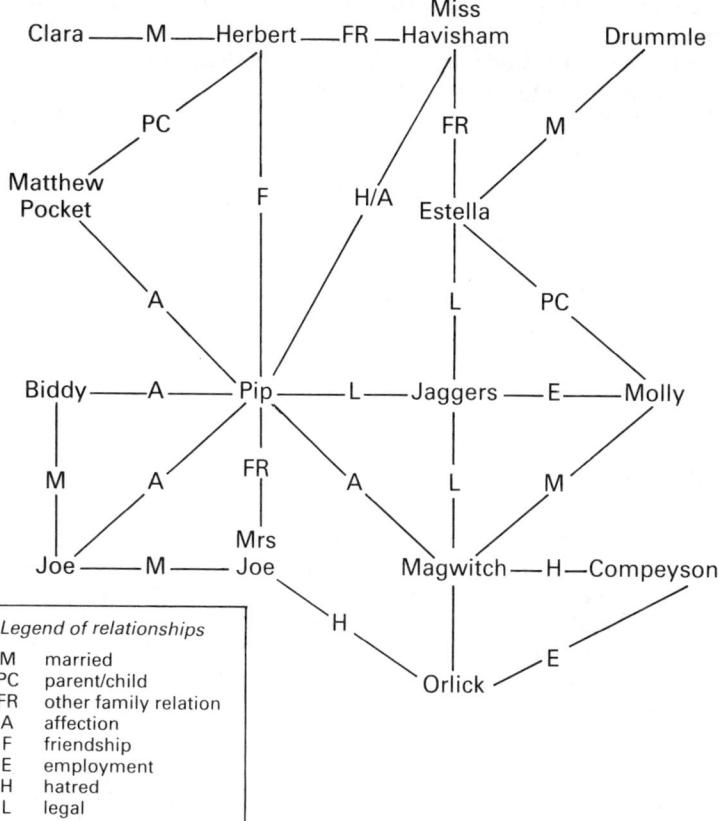

Legend of relationships

M	married
PC	parent/child
FR	other family relation
A	affection
F	friendship
E	employment
H	hatred
L	legal

Notes

1 The relationships shown belong to many different stages in the story. Some existed before the book begins; others come about as the plot develops.

2 All the relationships shown are mutual. One-way feelings, such as Pip's love for Estella, are not included.

3 Some characters, and even character groups (such as Wemmick's) are omitted.

4 Certain relationships (such as Compeyson–Miss Havisham) cannot be shown.

Figure 7 Taken from *Passing in Literature,* Roland Hindmarsh

5.1.3 *Games*

There are many games which can be played to reinforce information about a character e.g.:

Twenty Questions: Students are allowed 20 questions (to be answered by *Yes* or *No*) in which to guess the character.

Call My Bluff: Each team produces three comments which a character might have made, only one of which is genuine and the opposing team has to guess which one is correct. This is often helpful in making plain how writers use style markers to establish who is speaking in any particular text without actually naming the person.

> Can you think of any language games which could be adapted for work in the literature lesson?

5.2 Character and theme

Another of the ways in which the study of character can be approached is in relation to the theme. Consider *The Rover*, another of Conrad's works. There are perhaps two themes which stand out. The first is that of *Fraternity* or Brotherhood and the second that of *Manhood*. Conrad expands the first by contrasting the Brotherhood of the French Revolution with the Brotherhood of the Coast, the true friendship of the seamen highlighting the deficiencies of the mere political 'fraternité'. The second theme is worked out by measuring all the other men in the novel, such as Real, Scevola, Michel or the Cripple, against Peyrol, 'the man himself'.

The Cripple is a minor character, yet he is important because he serves to reinforce Conrad's point about true manhood. He assists Peyrol with the restoration of the boat and gets the villagers of Madrague to help him launch it. He thus earns Peyrol's respect and the comment 'C'est un homme ça' (That is a real man, that is). Peyrol is slightly scornful of Real, thinking that he has repressed all true feeling to the point where he is prepared to throw away his life and Arlette's happiness in the name of duty. He feels sorry for Michel the simpleton and has nothing but contempt for Scevola, the loyal citizen of the Revolution who has shed so much blood.

This relationship of character to theme can well be represented in a diagram, the students being encouraged to reflect on the different people's relationship to Peyrol and Conrad's reasons for including them.

A similar diagram could be established for the theme of Brotherhood.

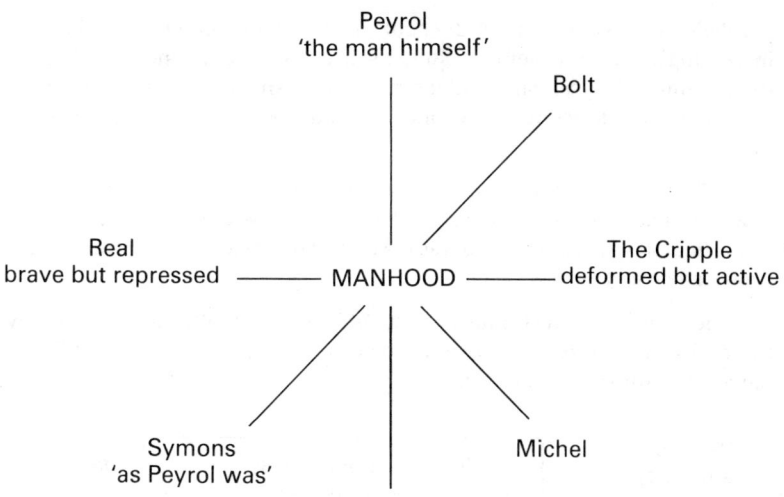

Peyrol
'the man himself'

Bolt

Real
brave but repressed ——— MANHOOD ——— The Cripple
deformed but active

Symons
'as Peyrol was'

Michel

Scevola, 'the blood drinker',
laughed at by the girls
of Madrague

5.3 Character and structure

Character study can also be used to demonstrate the structure of a novel, to illustrate why the author has chosen to reveal events and actions in the way he has. *The Rover* is typical of the way in which Conrad uses mystification to retain the reader's interest. Only little by little does the reader find out about Scevola and it is comparatively late in the book that one of the most significant facts about him is revealed. Before the Revolution he was regarded by the villagers as a comic and contemptible figure, laughed at by all the girls, and this explains why he is so attached to the revolutionary principle of equality.

The same is true of Arlette. The experiences which have affected her are withheld from the reader (who sees only that she appears half-crazed) until half-way through the book when she tells the Abbé about her part in the massacre at Toulon. Students might therefore keep a character index with events about the characters listed in chronological order. In this way they will be encouraged to reflect on why the author holds back certain information and what difference it makes to the reading when he does so.

Where development of character parallels the development of the story as a whole it is possible to represent the progress of the character in flow-chart form. In *Lord of the Flies*, for instance, the development of Roger's character parallels the development of the book; as the events on the island become increasingly more violent so Roger's actions become more and more unrestrained. His sadistic tendencies begin to show themselves when he starts to throw stones at Henry, one of the little boys, but dares not actually hit him:

> ... There was a space around Henry, perhaps six yards in diameter, into which he dare not throw. Here, invisible yet strong, was the taboo of the old life. Round the squatting child was the protection of parents and school and policemen and the law.

As time goes by the restraints of past authority gradually fall away and by the end of the story Roger has become the official torturer, 'wielding a nameless authority' of his own.

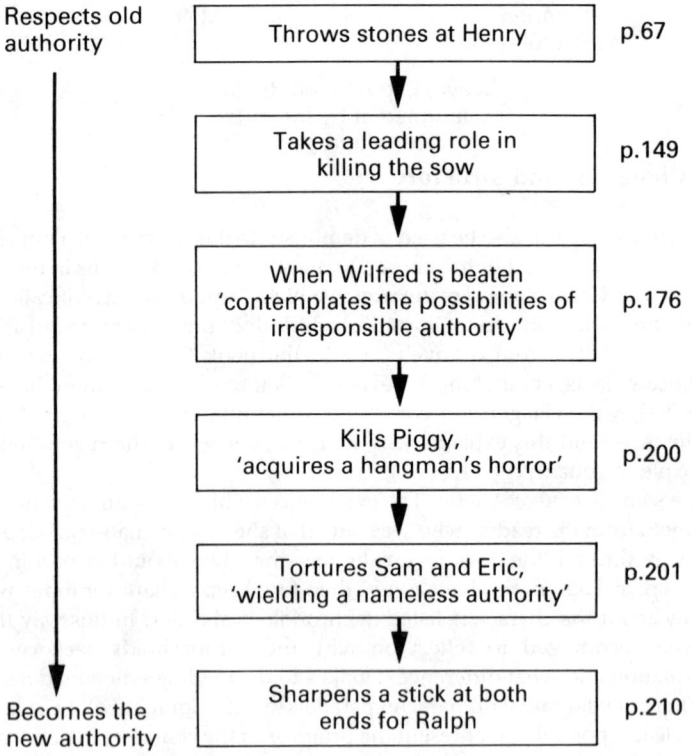

Respects old authority

| Throws stones at Henry | p.67 |

| Takes a leading role in killing the sow | p.149 |

| When Wilfred is beaten 'contemplates the possibilities of irresponsible authority' | p.176 |

| Kills Piggy, 'acquires a hangman's horror' | p.200 |

| Tortures Sam and Eric, 'wielding a nameless authority' | p.201 |

| Sharpens a stick at both ends for Ralph | p.210 |

Becomes the new authority

5.4 Character and language

5.4.1 *Vocabulary study*
Character can also be related to vocabulary study of one sort or another. Authors build up a picture of the characters they are describing by using language which evokes certain feelings and ideas in their readers. An exact grasp of the shades of meaning of the words they use is therefore important if the students are to understand fully the characters and their motives.

Initially such study might be a simple listing of new and useful vocabulary encountered. Students can check unknown words in the dictionary (for meaning and use rather than translation) and a discussion of the different shades of meaning can follow. In the vocabulary elicited about Mrs Harris's eyes, for example, the teacher might discuss what would happen if *wicked* were substituted for *naughty* in *naughty little eyes*. Can one differentiate between *roguish* and *saucy*, between *appraising*, *knowing* and *shrewd*?

Here it is not just a study of the words themselves but also of their *connotations*. The connotations are the area of association, suggestion and implication which surround a certain word, the ways in which it is coloured by the other words with which it is linked. Such vocabulary study as this, in addition to assisting students to appreciate the descriptions of people given, also contributes to their eventual grasp of the language generally and thereby plays a role in the functional approach to language teaching.

One way of highlighting the connotations of certain words is by the gap-filling exercise. Here, for example, is an extract adapted from *Flowers for Mrs Harris*, describing her reactions to the Dior dresses in Lady Dant's wardrobe.

Sample gap-filling exercise
It had all begun that day several years back when, during the course of her duties at Lady Dant's house, Mrs Harris had opened a wardrobe to tidy it and had come upon two dresses hanging there.

One was a bit of heaven in cream and ivory chiffon, the other an explosion in crimson ____1____ and taffeta, ____2____ great scarlet bows and a huge red ____3____. She stood there as though struck ____4____, for never in all her life had she seen anything quite as thrilling and ____5____.

____6____ and colourless as her existence would seem to have been, Mrs Harris had always felt a ____7____ for beauty and colour which up to this moment had manifested itself in a love for ____8____. She had the proverbial green ____9____ and as long as she had flowers Mrs Harris had no serious ____10____ about the life she led. Flowers were her escape from

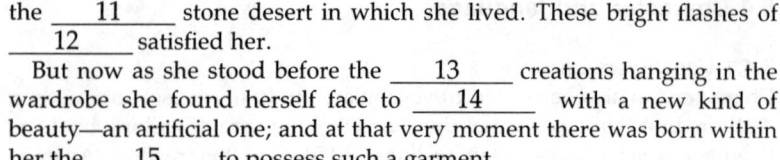

the ____11____ stone desert in which she lived. These bright flashes of
____12____ satisfied her.

But now as she stood before the ____13____ creations hanging in the
wardrobe she found herself face to ____14____ with a new kind of
beauty—an artificial one; and at that very moment there was born within
her the ____15____ to possess such a garment.

It can be seen that far fewer deletions are needed than for a readability cloze
test. The strictly numerical system of deletion has been abandoned and
items of stylistic interest have been removed instead. Later on this can be an
excellent springboard to critical analysis of an author's style as it encourages
students to think about the author's intentions. Why, when all of the words
that they had suggested were suitable, did he pick *that* one.

Not only will the students gain an extra insight into Mrs Harris's
character, and gain the courage needed to face a drab existence without
complaint, but they will also exercise their knowledge of the language.
Deletions 4, 9 and 14, for example, will check on their knowledge of certain
idiomatic expressions: *struck dumb*, *green fingers* and *face to face*. All the
adjectives used to describe the dresses provide an interesting semantic area
for the students to explore: *stunning*, *beautiful*, *thrilling*, *a bit of heaven*. So too
do their opposites, the words used to describe Mrs Harris's existence: *drab*
and *colourless*, in a *sombre* stone desert. Obviously the Thesaurus would be
of use to students trying this exercise. The discussion amongst themselves
of the different connotations of each word (shall it be *dull*, *drab* or
disinteresting for 6, for example) should provoke considerable vocabulary
awareness. Much will depend in exercises of this type on the teacher's
picking the right passage and selecting the most worthwhile items to delete.

Another facet of connotation is that some words are associated with
disapproval while some indicate approval. An author can thus make his
own attitude towards the character plain without direct comment. In *The
Loved One*, for example, Waugh's opinion of Mr Joyboy is signalled by the
words he uses to describe him physically: the *unathletic* body, *scant*
eyebrows and *fleshy* hands. Fleshy, for instance, with its overtones of
unhealthy fatness and flabbiness, is always used in a pejorative sense as
contrasted with *plump*, a word of similar meaning, but which can be
attractive. Exercises such as those below can assist students to become
aware of such connotations.

Exercise A
Fill in the missing words on the grid below:

	Good	Neutral	Bad
1	Persevering	Persistent	Stubborn
2		Fat	Fleshy
3		Smell	

Exercise B
Arrange the following words in a series going from the most derogatory through the most neutral to the most pleasant:
1 Obese, overweight, fleshy, plump, outsize, fat
2 Shrewd, perceptive, calculating, knowing, appraising
3 Male, manly, virile, macho, unfeminine

Exercise C
Find the inappropriate word in each of the sentences which follow:
1 The fragrance of the rubbish heap makes me feel ill.
2 Hitler was a meglomaniac, a sadist and told fibs.
3 Ladies and gentlemen, we are gathered together today to hear the Bishop chat about brass-rubbing.

Some excellent exercises of this type can be found in *The Words You Need* (Rudzka et al. 1981). Such exercises should help students crystallise the semantic area of any particular word and therefore sharpen their view of the character it is describing—literature study and advanced vocabulary studying working hand in hand.

5.4.2 *Varieties of English*
As command of the language grows students will be able increasingly to appreciate how characters can be marked by the language they use. Some might have a highly latinate vocabulary and their degree of education might be assumed from their use of words of more than two syllables. Advanced students might compare, for example, the differences in speech between Manuel and the Marquesa de Montemayor in Thornton Wilder's *The Bridge of San Luis Rey*.

As time goes on students will realise that people's ways of expression often fall into certain registers which serve to mark them.

Register

Clearly the subject under discussion is of great importance in a person's decision as to how he or she will speak. No one expects a scientific talk to be expressed in the same language as an informal chat. Language varies as its function varies and the name given to a variety of language distinguished by its use is register.

Often a subject will produce its own jargon: we have the language of bureaucracy or 'red tape', journalese in newspapers or the legal language of the Courts. Obviously a judge speaks in a different way when he is on the bench to the way he speaks in ordinary life but often flavours of the legal language creep into his everyday vocabulary.

Take the lawyer, Mr Sandal, for example, in *Brat Farrar*, a book by Josephine Tey about a young man called Brat who pretends to be Patrick Ashby, the missing heir to the estate of the wealthy Ashby family. When Brat in the guise of Patrick is interviewed by Mr Sandal in the presence of Bee Ashby, Patrick's aunt, the lawyer says:

> Miss Ashby is no doubt <u>prepared to vouch for</u> <u>you</u>, but you will understand that the matter needs more clarification. If it were a simple matter of a prodigal's homecoming your aunt's acceptance of you would no doubt be sufficient to restore you to the bosom of your family. But <u>in the present instance</u> it is a <u>matter of property.</u> Of the ultimate destination of a fortune. And <u>the law will require incontrovertible evidence</u> of your identity before you could be allowed to succeed to anything that was Patrick Ashby's. I hope you understand our position.'

All the underlined words stress the fact that Mr Sandal is a lawyer and that he chooses his words with care, as lawyers must.

As the students' acquaintance with the English language broadens they will become aware of these different registers. The teacher can set a series of exercises of the type below to help them become more familiar with the most common ones which they may come across.

Sample exercise

In what context would you expect to find the following types of language?
1 Heat the wet ingredients together and add with the egg to the flour and ginger. Beat thoroughly and pour into a greased tin.
2 Large, spacious town house, two bathrooms, central heating, dining/lounge area 270 square feet, own garage in rear block.
3 Dearly beloved, we are gathered here this day to remember our dear friend, husband and father, Elisha Smith.

4   The driver of the car should check his rear-view mirror and signal his intention to turn in sufficient time to warn any following vehicle of this intention.

An awareness of the different registers available to speakers will help them appreciate what is going on when an author caricatures a certain register, as Evelyn Waugh makes fun of journalistic jargon in *Scoop*. Once the students know what to look for they often enjoy tracking down such stylistic markers.

Ranges of formality

Another area in which characters can be marked is in the formality of their expression. This is particularly important in works where the theme lies in the clash of social class. The different levels of formality used help to maintain the distinction between the upper and working class people. The novels of L P Hartley, such as *The Go-between* and *The Hireling*, demonstrate vividly the subtle interplay of across-class speech.

In *The Hireling* Leadbitter, a car-hire driver, is engaged to take Lady Franklin to a Cathedral:

'This is Lady Franklin's butler speaking,' he was told. 'Her ladyship wishes to know if you can take her ladyship to Canterbury on Thursday, February 10th. Her ladyship would be starting at 10.30 in the morning and would be returning in the late afternoon.'

What a lot of ladyships, Leadbitter thought. He glanced at his engagement list which he kept in a large, florid silver photograph frame beside the telephone. It had once enshrined the picture of the woman with whom he had lived longest, and was almost the only momento of his past life that he had allowed himself.

'Yes, I can do that. Where shall I pick her up?'

'Pick her ladyship up?' The butler sounded shocked. 'Will you call for her at her residence, 39 South Halkin Street.'

In using the phrase *pick her up* Leadbitter is using language to the butler, who is his equal, that he would not have used to Lady Franklin herself. The butler maintains his very formal mode of address (*what a lot of ladyships*, thinks Leadbitter) in order to indicate his superiority to the car hire driver but, in fact, it only serves to make him sound faintly ridiculous.

Formality is often used by an author to indicate that an older person is speaking, one belonging to an era when people were generally more formal in their modes of address. In the quotation from *Brat Farrar*, for example, Mr Sandal refers to Bee as Miss Ashby after many years acquaintance.

One of the best ways to establish with the students the differences implicit in varying degrees of formality is to underline the types of vocabulary and structures liable to be used in formal or informal situations. This can be accomplished by a series of exercises similar to that below:

Arrange the following utterances in the most likely order of occurrence.
Car park attendant to driver:
(a) Over in the corner please.
(b) Could you please park over there, sir.
(c) Over there.
(d) Would you please park over there.
(e) Put that heap of metal over there, out of the way.

From there the students could progress to acting out simple role-play situations between people where differing degrees of formality would be appropriate e.g.:

pupil to teacher
road traffic offender to policeman
customer to sales lady
householder to tramp

They would soon realise that not only does one's speech vary when talking to different types of people but also one's stance and whole attitude. Once again the relationship of communicative language teaching to literature study is very close. (See Chapter 3 on setting up role-play situations.)

5.4.3 *Slang, idiolect and dialect*

At the other end of the formality scale are slang and colloquial speech, both of which can be very potent in the portrayal of character. The speech of ordinary people is often marked by well-worn expressions or clichés as well as by the more obvious slang of certain groups.

When Leadbitter is speaking to Lady Franklin about her husband's death he says: 'I expect his heart just *conked out*' and tries to console her by saying '*There's no use crying over spilt milk*'. While neither of these remarks in particular mark Leadbitter as belonging to a certain class and having a certain background the frequency of his use of such expressions does, and the teacher can get students to note the clichés and slang expressions when they occur.

Where people use a very distinctive sort of speech marked by particular turns of phrase or lexis this is referred to as their idiolect. Pistol, the low life friend of Falstaff in *Henry V*, employs overblown and pretentious language, filled with foreign phrases, which he uses as often as not, incorrectly. In this way Shakespeare has 'marked' his character.

Colloquial speech, often associated with dialect, is also used by an author to give life to the characters. Occasionally dialect is used to denote worthiness (faithful retainers often speak in dialect) and is sometimes reserved for lesser or comic characters. Students need to be aware of these connotations.

In order to assist students to cope with dialect the teacher should provide some help with the various conventions of phrase and spelling associated with dialect speech. Cockney *was*, for example, is often written *woz* even though pronounced in more or less the same way as the correct form. It is obviously helpful for the students to hear tapes of authentic dialect speakers (a recording of *Wuthering Heights*, for example, would assist students to cope with the Yorkshire dialect).

It can be seen that a study of character can lead students on to a study, not only of descriptive language, but also of speech in context. Literature and language study in this sense work together, both benefiting the students in their efforts to understand the way communication is opened up and maintained.

6 Approach to text—Structure

Once the students have come to as full an understanding of the content and characterisation as possible they are ready to pursue the next line of investigation, that of form. The notion of form may be related to either structural or textural procedures, structure being the large scale matter of the arrangement or ordering of a work, texture referring to matters of immediate impression. The plot, story or stanza form might therefore be said to relate to the structure or framework of the text and the diction, syntax, imagery and rhythms to the texture. Both constitute what is sometimes referred to as the author's style (Roway 1982).

6.1 Structure and the novel

At the beginning of their course the students are likely to have been considering 'realistic' texts where the author is aiming for factual, objective reportage. The ordering is liable to be chronological, the style unobtrusive. As time goes on, however, they will be set works of a more complex nature and questions of structure will become more important. Authors have used a variety of methods to 'construct' their works and students will wish to investigate some of these.

6.1.1 *Sequencing*
In considering some of the more complex works it becomes evident that there are more ways of arranging the material than simply in strict, chronological order and that the structure of a book or play depends not only on what incidents the author chooses to tell but also those he omits. Sometimes it is what we are not told that heightens our interest. Sometimes the author will choose to take an incident out of order, either moving forward or backward in the time sequence followed by the story, to intrigue us and keep us reading on.

In *The Bridge of San Luis Rey*, the book starts with a description of the breaking of the bridge and the deaths of the five people who fall from it, but it does not say who the five are. The following chapters revert to the time before the bridge breaks and tell, in a series of flashbacks, the stories of each of those who are killed and of the people related to them.

The teacher can ask the students *why* the author has chosen to reveal in advance that some of the characters will die. It should not be difficult to elicit the idea that the technique has been used to arouse and then heighten the reader's interest. As we read about the various characters in the book we are aware that some of them must die but since we are not sure who we are kept on tenterhooks.

How can we make sure that students are following in cases where structure is not straightforward? If the order is not chronological they can draw up a list of events in the order in which they occur in the book with the page numbers for reference. After the first reading has been accomplished they can sort these events out into the correct time order as a sort of story index. Such indexes should be very brief (not more than one sentence to each event) to enable them to have the whole novel in view and see it in its true proportions. They will have to be written up after the reading in order for the students to be sure which sections are relevant to the main flow of events and which characters are important to the plot. Although the Bishop of Lima, for example, figures very prominently on the first page of *The Bridge of San Luis Rey* he is not one of the principal characters whose actions affect the story.

This method of out-of-sequence presentation is much used by Joseph Conrad and in *The Rover* he frequently departs from the natural time order to recall the past or anticipate the future. The main events of the book actually extend over a comparatively short space of time, from Saturday night to the following Monday, and it is these events that the students will need to note down chronologically. The main outline would look something like the one below and they would then be able to flesh it out with such details as they find of importance.

Sample Story Index for *The Rover*

Saturday
1   Bolt and his men land from the Amelia to investigate the Escampobar farm.
2   Symons visits Peyrol's boat and is imprisoned there.

Sunday
1   Peyrol and Real develop their plan for deceiving the English.
2   Symons is allowed to escape and returns to the Amelia.
3   Scevola is imprisoned on the boat.

Monday
1   Peyrol knocks out Real and sails off with Michael and Scevola.

2 They are killed by the English.

In the book this is all presented piecemeal and the readers allowed only gradual insight into the characters' motives and occupations. The effect of this jigsaw method of presentation is to arouse the reader's curiosity to a high pitch. Various pieces of the jigsaw, when finally inserted, provide the overall picture; events and motives slot into place.

The same is true of structure at paragraph as well as story level and a variety of sequencing exercises can be introduced to help students become aware of such structural techniques.

Jigsaw methods

1 Give them a list similar to the story index above, arranged in random order, and have them decide in groups on the correct order. Allow for a session at the end for them to compare notes.

2 Divide a chapter or part of a chapter into sections, each section ending, if possible, at a dramatic point or at one where what will happen next is uncertain. Give each group a section copied onto a separate piece of paper and instruct them to read it silently. The group then discusses what has happened in their section and what they think might have happened in the story before and after the section they have just read. The class together then decide in what order the sections must have come in the original story.

> What five sections could you select from Chapter 1 of *The Rover* to use as a jigsaw reading exercise?

3 Several consecutive sentences of a passage are rearranged in random order and the students, working in groups, have to put the sentences back into an order that makes sense. In performing this task the students have to focus on punctuation and typographical clues, syntax and units of meaning, the logic of the author's argument, the way in which the pronouns refer back and so on.

Sample extract from *Animal Farm*

1 One night there was a loud crash in the yard, and the animals rushed out of their stalls.

2 It was a moonlight night.

3 At the foot of the end wall of the big barn, where the Seven Commandments were written, there lay a ladder broken in two pieces.

4 Squealer, temporarily stunned, was sprawling beside it, and near at hand there lay a lantern, a paintbrush and an overturned pot of white paint.

5 The dogs immediately made a ring round Squealer and escorted him back to the farmhouse as soon as he was able to walk.

6 None of the animals could form any idea as to what this meant, except old Benjamin, who nodded his muzzle with a knowing air, and seemed to understand but would say nothing.

7 But a few days later Muriel, reading over the Seven Commandments to herself noticed that there was yet another of them which the animals had remembered wrong.

8 They had thought that the Fifth Commandment was 'No animal shall drink alcohol', but there were two words that they had forgotten.

9 Actually the Commandment read: 'No animal shall drink alcohol to excess.'

In this extract, the position of all the sentences, with the possible exception of 2, is dictated by the narrative and laws of cohesion (see Chapter 7). With other passages it is not so easy to decide on the correct order.

Work out the original order of the sentences below taken from Evelyn Waugh's *The Loved One*:

1 Dennis hesitated with his fingers on the handle and was aware of communication with another hand beyond the panels.

2 At the moment of their meeting a treble voice broke out with a poignant sweetness: 'O for the Wings of a Dove'.

3 No breath stirred the enchanted stillness of the two rooms.

4 The leaded casements were screwed tight.

5 Thus in a hundred novels had lovers stood quite close to him; behind her more, many more flowers and all about her a rich hot-house scent and the low voices of a choir discoursing sacred music from the cornice.

6 The air came, like the boy's voice, from far away, sterilized and transmuted.

7 'Come in, Mr Barlow.'

8 The temperature was slightly cooler than is usual in American dwellings.

9 The rooms seemed isolated and unnaturally quiet, like a railway coach that has stopped in the night far from any station.

Frequently, students decide that several orderings are acceptable without the overall meaning being appreciably altered. It then becomes obvious, once the author's original arrangement has been consulted, that there are more ways of organising material other than by simply putting down the events in chronological order. The teacher can then go on to discuss points of sentence length, balance and rhythm and this can all lead to a fruitful analysis of how effects are achieved in writing.

6.1.2 Themes

Another way of approaching the structure of a text is to consider the ideas and preoccupations which run throughout it, the themes which give it unity, and the reasons why the author has included some incidents and not others.

Things Fall Apart by Chinua Achebe, for example, is a carefully structured and tightly wrought novel in which the personal tragedy of Okonkwo, the hero of the book is closely interwoven with the breakdown of Ibo society as a whole after the coming of the white man. The teacher's aim will be to ensure that the students are aware of those two themes, that the book is concerned not only with Okonkwo's individual tragedy, destroyed by his own pre-disposition to violence and his inability to adapt to the new ways, but also with the tragedy of the whole race.

It is necessary though for the students to discover these themes and their significance on their own. Only by their finding out for themselves the ideas and associated emotions underlying the text will they be able to relate to them and come to an understanding of the ways in which a work can communicate with the reader.

To enable them to make these discoveries on their own requires some ingenuity on the part of the teacher. A series of 'leading questions' of some kind will need to be set which not only guide the students to the underlying themes of the work, but show them how to trace such themes for themselves.

In order, for example, to draw the students' attention to the ways in which Achebe has interwoven the theme of the disintegration of clan life with Okonkwo's story choose four different aspects of clan life to discuss with them. These can be:

1 the religious system
2 the legal system
3 clan law on twins
4 the unity of the clan.

Divide the class into four groups, each of which will discuss one of those four aspects. They can be given a set of questions relating to their theme and, to save time, some indication of where the answers might be found, e.g.:

Group 1 (Religion)

(a) What sort of religion did the villagers have? What was the iyi-uwa and what was the effect of finding it on the family? What happened to Ezinma when Chielo took her? (Part I, 9–11, 69–77, 93–99)

(b) What do the villagers expect to happen when the Christians build their church in the Evil Forest? What happens to the man who is believed to have killed the sacred python? What sort of people become Christians at first? (Part II, 135–6, 147, 142)

(c) Which titled man becomes a Christian and why? What do the villagers believe has happened when the Egwugwu is unmasked? What do they do about it? What happens to them? (Part III, 157, 168, 172, 173–176).

The answers to those questions and those set to the other groups should reveal the way in which Achebe has shaped his novel and can be set out in the following way.

OLD ORDER	TRANSITIONAL PERIOD	NEW ORDER
1 Practice ancestor worship. Finding the iyi-uwa, a special stone, vindicates their belief. Ezinma is rescued from death and devoted to the God.	Allow missionaries into Evil Forest. They are expected to die but do not. The killer of the python dies. Only unworthy people become Christians.	A titled man, Ogbuefi Ugonna, becomes a Christian. Villagers believe one of the ancestral spirits has been killed when the Egwugwu is unmasked. They burn down the Church but are imprisoned themselves.
2 Legal matters are settled by the Egwugwu. Murder of Udo's wife in Mbaino is settled by payment of compensation and the eventual death of Ekemefuna.	All the villagers of Abame are killed for the death of one white man.	Aneto's land case is settled unjustly due to the white man's ignorance of Ibo language and customs.
3 Twin are exposed in the forest.	Nneka, mother of twins, becomes a Christian. Christians save twins.	New law forbids killing of twins.
4 United in action over Udo's wife. All villagers are present.	Elder complains of disunity at Okonkwo's final feast in Mbanta.	Villagers do not all come to the final meeting and do not support Okonkwo against the Court Messenger.

Figure 8

It should become evident how the book is structured. Each of the three parts into which it is divided reflects a stage in the clan's life and eventual distintegration. The teacher might illustrate this by the diagram below:

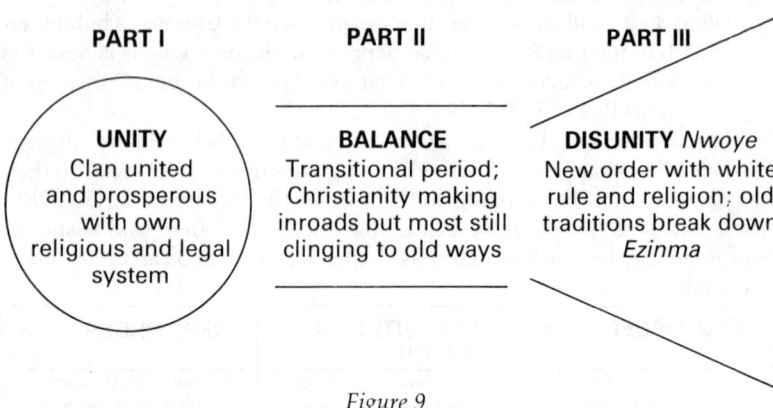

PART I	PART II	PART III
UNITY Clan united and prosperous with own religious and legal system	**BALANCE** Transitional period; Christianity making inroads but most still clinging to old ways	**DISUNITY** *Nwoye* New order with white rule and religion; old traditions break down *Ezinma*

Figure 9

The students can extend the list above with parallels of their own once they have caught the general idea. Groups can be required to choose a passage related to their theme which they consider to be the most important to read aloud to the class. They can set questions on their own theme in the same way. The relationship of Ezinma and Nwoye, two of Okonkwo's children, to the main theme of the book can be studied, Ezinma being devoted to the God and Nwoye becoming a Christian and going away to teacher training college at the end.

In these ways they should come to recognise the structural importance of themes, the fact that they can serve as a link between what might seem totally unrelated incidents, and create an underlying framework for the text.

6.1.3 *Foreshadowing*
Another common technique, already mentioned in Chapter 3, is to insert events or descriptions into the main body of the text which can be seen, in retrospect, to foreshadow the main events which make up the climax of the novel. Once again the problem is to get the students to find the 'clues' for themselves.

In the case of *Things Fall Apart* it is evident that Okonkwo's killing of the messenger and his subsequent suicide are the culmination of the events reported in the novel. Asked why Okonkwo killed the messenger and then himself the students will probably be able to suggest the idea that it is his own hasty temper and his desire to do the 'manly' thing which has caused his downfall, as well as his disillusionment with the breakdown in the old way of life and his inability to cope with the new ways.

Having been informed that there are clues as to what might happen earlier in the book the students can go through trying to find the ways in which Achebe has forewarned the reader that something of this nature might occur. Once again they can be divided into groups with certain sections to consider so that too much time is not taken up on the search. Afterwards they can compare notes and should be able to produce a list similar to the one below:

1 Okonkwo is the first to bring home a human head from the war.
2 He beats his wife in temper in Peace week and will not stop 'even for the gods'.
3 He shoots at his wife because she implies he is a poor hunter.
4 He takes part in the death of Ekemefuna against the advice of Ezeudu.
5 He kills Ezeudu's son by accident.
6 He takes part in the burning of the church.

Given assistance of this sort the students will eventually realise the kinds of technique an author uses to bind his work together and make it coherent and will begin to search for the 'clues' themselves.

6.2 Structure and drama

Playwrights also make use of such techniques as sequencing, fore-shadowing (sometimes a form of dramatic irony, and the withholding of certain information to structure their work.) In *An Inspector Calls*, for example, J B Priestly reveals only gradually that each member of the family was involved with the girl who committed suicide, using the technique of the police interview to hold certain information back.

The structure of a play is, perhaps, more easily visible to the students in that the skeleton or framework of the text is partly provided by the division into acts and scenes. The dramatist has to get his characters on and off the stage and this provides natural breaks in the action. It helps students to know that the climax or pivotal scene usually comes in the second act of a three act play and the third act of a five act play (e.g. Caesar's death in Act III, Sc. i of *Julius Caesar*, marks the point for Brutus when there is no turning back and is followed by the famous scene where both Brutus and Antony talk to the crowd).

One of the first tasks of a dramatist is to convince us that what we see on the stage is 'real', to enable us to 'suspend our disbelief'. There are, however, a variety of constraints upon them which work against this 'reality' and so several different conventions have been adopted to help make the action on stage seem more credible.

6.2.1 Constraints and conventions

Time is a constraint upon the playwright since he must compress his story into what is usually no more than an evening's entertainment for the spectator. He cannot require the events of the story to take place in many different geographical locations because of the problems with scene changing. The actual size and limitations of the stage will also restrict him since there are certain events which are almost impossible to represent adequately in a small area.

In the play *Equus* by Peter Shaeffer, for example, a young man blinds six horses and the play consists of his interviews with the psychiatrist trying to discover the root of his problems and flashbacks to events leading up to the blinding. It would obviously be impractical, if not impossible, to have six horses on stage night after night. Schaeffer turns the constraint to a virtue by having actors wearing horse masks take the parts of the horses, creating thereby a memorable piece of visual imagery and pointing up the symbolic role of the horses. It is easy to see, however, that the credibility of the play is put at risk, by such methods, that there is a danger that the audience will not 'join the game' and will not 'suspend their disbelief'.

These constraints have therefore led to the conventions of the three Unities, those of Time, Place and Action, originally introduced from Greek religious drama.

- Unity of Time dictated that all the action should take place within a limited period usually one of no more than 24 hours.
- Unity of Place dictated that the action should all take place in one geographical area.
- Unity of Action dictated that all events should be directly related to the main plot and be homogeneous in tone, i.e. either tragic or comic but not both. All violent action was to take place off stage.

Some plays have been written which adhere absolutely to these principles, but clearly many famous works disregard them to a greater or lesser extent.

Students can explore the ways in which the constraints have influenced an author's choice in constructing his work. They can, for example, consider what shifts he is put to to familiarise the audience with the background to his story while introducing the plot at the same time.

> *Task*: Study the first two scenes of *The Tempest*, a play in which
> Shakespeare came as close to respecting the Unities as he ever did.
> How does he let the audience know the way in which Prospero came
> to the island and what his relationship is to the shipwrecked people?

Students can make lists of the changes which would be possible if the work they are studying were presented on film rather than on the stage. Certain events (e.g. the funeral of Willy Loman in Miller's *Death of a Salesman*) would undoubtedly receive fuller treatment in a novel or film. The compression of the action in a play, however, makes for greater intensity, a heightening of emotion, and thereby contributes to the play's impact.

Another convention of Greek drama was the Chorus, enabling the author himself to comment on the action and guide the audience's attention in one way or another. In *Murder in the Cathedral* T S Eliot uses the device of a chorus to make plain Beckett's dilemma. Often dramatists use the device more obliquely, inserting minor characters into the plot who can comment on the action for the author or whose actions themselves provide an apt contrast to those of the main character.

Touchstone, for example, in Shakespeare's *As You Like It* represents an earthy commentary on the romantic goings-on at the Duke's court and his peasant antics parallel the actions of the Duke's entourage, pointing up the affectations of the nobles. Students could therefore draw up a list of Touchstone's comments on 'courtly' subjects with appropriate quotations:

On Poetry: I'll rhyme you so eight years together, dinners and suppers and sleeping hours excepted: it is a right butterwoman's rank to market.

On Marriage: As the ox hath his bow, sir, the horse his curb and the falcon her bells, so man hath his desires: and as pigeons bill, so wedlock would be nibbling.

They should then be able to observe that Touchstone serves to prick the sentimental bubble that surrounds the nobles and brings the work 'down to earth'.

6.3 Structure and poetry

When discussing poetry students will certainly have talked about form to a limited extent early on, identifying a poem as a ballad or sonnet perhaps and working out the rhyme scheme. With more advanced students it should be possible to discuss the appropriateness of that form.

Sample text *The Red Wheelbarrow* by William Carlos Williams

Aim: to demonstrate that the way a poem is designed and laid out is inextricably part of the work and cannot be changed without subtly altering the content

> *The Red Wheelbarrow*
>
> So much depends
> upon
>
> a red wheel
> barrow
>
> glazed with rain
> water
>
> beside the white
> chickens.

The poem is about the way people see things, that fact that although we look at things to identify them we rarely pay any real attention to them. And so it makes us look at familiar objects with new eyes, makes us aware of the peculiar intrinsic qualities of what we see around us. The problem is to get the students to see how William Carlos Williams achieves this. There is, of course, no single way of looking at a poem, but the following exercise should direct the students's attention to the structure and its effect.

Exercise on *The Red Wheelbarrow*:

1 Write down the compound words and collocations (words which would normally be together) which have been split.
   Answer: depends upon, wheelbarrow, rainwater, white chickens
2 Write down the adjectives and descriptive phrases used in the poem.
   Answer: red, glazed with rain, white
3 Rewrite the poem as one straightforward sentence.
   Answer: So much depends upon a red wheelbarrow, glazed with rainwater, beside the white chickens.

It should become evident that the effect of the unorthodox arrangement of the words in the poem is to slow things down and stress the separateness of the objects, the barrow, the water, the chickens, each of which has a line to itself. The readers are forced to look at the poem as they would at a painting, seeing the individual parts of it, their eyes moving back and forth over the scene, the red wheelbarrow gleaming in the rain and the white chickens.

This poem is initially a little obscure, however, (What exactly depends on the red wheelbarrow?) and is unorthodox in both structure and punctuation (e.g. there are no capitals). It is possible, though, to discuss poems which are severely traditional in style and demonstrate that the form is not merely a conventional container for the content but also profoundly influences it. *Piazza piece* by John Crowe Ransome is such a poem and is considered in detail in Chapter 8.

6.3.1 *Structuralist Criticism*
It is possible to consider any text in relation to the form of the work and the author's intention rather than as a poem, play or story in its own right.

In a discussion of *Jane Eyre* by Charlotte Bronte, for example, instead of concentrating the students' attention on Jane herself, encouraging them to look at her as a 'real' person, the teacher would rather direct their attention to Charlotte Bronte and her style. They might investigate the way in which she has structured the work and used certain vocabulary and incidents; how her attitude and purpose in writing has influenced the reader's view of Jane; and thus how the language has created an illusion of 'reality'.

There is a branch of modern criticism referred to as *structuralist criticism* which goes even further than this. Followers of this approach (of whom the original exponents were Roland Barthes and Jacques Derrida) insist that there is no reality, that texts are merely 'games with verbal counters' and writing a 'trick of language and preconceptions brought to the text by the reader' (Rodway 1982). Obviously criticism at this level is beyond the scope of this book and even discussion of structure in a more general way needs to be embarked upon by teachers with extreme care. They should be sure that the students can understand.

7 Approach to text—Style and purpose

Once the students have a clear overall view of the work the teacher should be able to discuss the finer points of the author's style with them. As with structure, however, it will often only be possible with advanced students.

All writers, in choosing the language they will use must take into account three factors: the subject, their anticipated audience and their purpose in writing. Their style will reflect those factors and students making a critical survey of their texts will need to consider the various techniques they have used to attain their ends and make judgements on how well they have achieved them.

Is a particular point plain, for example? Why did the writer choose this word over other possibilities? Is the language vivid, clear and appropriate? Or is it possible that the author is striving for obscurity, hoping to convey his or her thoughts by impression rather than realism, by what the painters call chiaroscuro, or the art of shading?

The study of style, therefore, is the study of language in context, the way that the language chosen expresses the author's purpose. The links between the story and the way the author has described it can be expressed in diagram form:

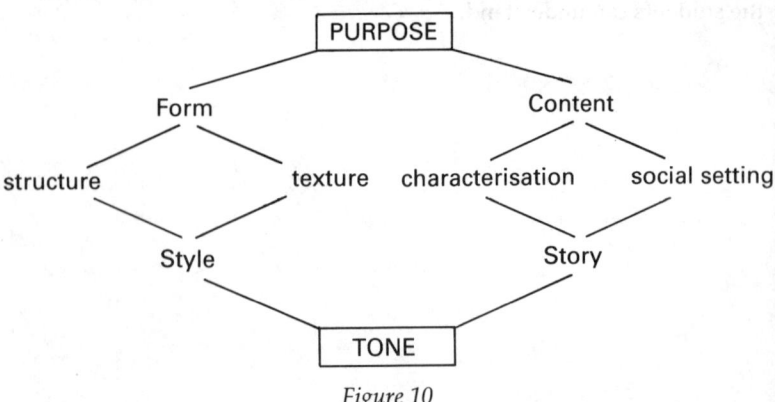

Figure 10

7.1 Areas of Study

The areas covered by stylistic analysis are many and can be related to lexical features, internal structure, figures of speech the discourse situation or the tone of the work as a whole.

7.1.1 *Lexical features*

Any vocabulary study should enable the students to perceive the functions and range of the lexis as well as the aptness of certain words in context. From the start the teacher should encourage the students to invest in the necessary tools for vocabulary study: a good monolingual dictionary, such as Longman's *Dictionary of Contemporary English* or the *Macmillan Student's Dictionary*, a notebook for recording words or phrases that need comment or remembering and, for more advanced students, a Thesaurus of some kind. A Thesaurus will reveal not just a simple explanation of the meaning of the word but enough examples to make clear the *range* of the lexis associated with a given concept. Advanced students should also have access to a good etymological dictionary.

Words may be analysed individually as
- abstract or concrete
- learned or common
- simple or complex

or they may figure as parts of a greater unit as in compounds, collocations or idioms. Different varieties of English can be considered:
- the register (e.g. scientific, religious or legal language)
- the range of formality (very formal, colloquial, slang)
- the area of difference between spoken and written language.

Often an individual word will not, of itself, indicate a particular register but its collocation with another will. *Right* is presumably neutral as is *a hook*, but *a right hook* can only come from the boxing world.

7.1.2 *Internal structure*

This generally refers to the *cohesion* of the passage, the way in which the various parts relate to each other and to the work as a whole. Such cohesion can be achieved by a variety of devices such as:
- lexical repetition of various kinds
- use of pronouns for cross-reference
- use of logical links such as *however*, *thus* and *therefore*.

Some good examples of how cohesions works and a variety of exercises to assist students can be found in *Reading in the Language Classroom* (Williams

1984:75–81). The jigsaw sequencing exercises described in Chapter 6 (pp 74-76) can also help students understand how cohesion helps to make the text coherent.

7.1.3 *Figurative language*
Figurative language is language that is *marked* or *foregrounded* (made to stand out) by its departure from the general norms of communication. Such departures can be by:

- repetition
- deviation.

Structural and lexical repetition, for example, can produce parallelisms where one half of the sentence balances the other half (e.g. *They have sown the wind, they shall reap the whirlwind*). Phonological repetition can produce rhyme and alliteration which occurs when consonants at the start of consecutive or near consecutive words are repeated (e.g. Five *m*iles *m*eandering with a *m*azy *m*otion). Lexical deviation may lead to new words being formed (e.g. Golding's *flinked*), strange collocations or the traditional figures of speech such as metaphor and paradox, which depend for their effects on the joining of unexpected language features.

7.1.4 *Discourse situation*
The discourse situation or context of a work is related to the network of relationships built up between the author, the reader and the characters involved in the story:

- author to reader—does the writer address the reader directly, guiding him in this direction or that? Does he use an 'I' persona or a character to give his opinion of the situation?
- author to character—does the author seem to be in sympathy with the character, does he look at the world from the character's point of view?
- character to character—do we appear to be able to see inside the minds of both characters or only of one, do we identify with one character as opposed to another?
- author to narrator—is the narrator different from the author, i.e. does he hold different attitudes and values to the author and if so, how can we deduce this?

All of these relationships depend to some extent on common knowledge and assumptions shared by the author and reader.

7.1.5 *Tone*
The tone of a text is closely related to its *mode*, whether, for example, it can be categorised as fictional or factual, tragic or comic. Such considerations

will dictate, to a large extent, the 'atmosphere' or tone of the work. People trying to write factually, for example, do not usually have an obtrusive style, nor use highly figurative language.

The line between fact and fiction is not fixed, as Capote's *In Cold Blood* and Keneally's *Schindler's Ark* (works of fiction based on fact) have shown. Texts do not often fall neatly into one category or another. If, however, students can label a text in some way, either realistic or impressionistic, tragic or comic and so on, they will have made a start in coming to terms with it critically.

Can you categorise the following texts in some way or other?

Othello (Shakespeare)	*Wuthering Heights* (Bronte)
The Importance of Being Earnest (Wilde)	*Nostromo* (Conrad)
The Merchant of Venice (Shakespeare)	*Gulliver's Travels* (Swift)
Ulysses (Joyce)	*A House for Mr Biswas* (Naipaul)

A very comprehensive list of the various stylistic categories which might be considered is given in *Style in Fiction* (Leech and Short 1981) along with examples of analysis of a variety of texts.

7.2 Concrete tasks

One of the major problems in analysing an author's style is the amount of subjectivity that enters into any assessment of another person's command of the language. I, for example, may quite like this particular style: my students may not. There is also the disparity between the English taught for use abroad and the language used in Britain. Passages in working class language and full of local idiom, for example, might seem very down to earth and simple to a native speaker but very complicated to a foreign learner who has not the same feel for the way ordinary English people use the language. Conversely, language which might seem overblown or pretentious to an English person might not seem so to someone whose mother tongue is rich in hyperbole and ornate expression and who is liable to have learned the formal word or expression before the informal.

It is therefore better to choose stylistic elements which can be analysed by the students themselves, performing concrete tasks, rather than concentrate on those which are subjectively impressionistic (Enkvist, Spencer and Gregory 1964:7).

This can be illustrated by an analysis of the following text.

Sample text from *To the Lighthouse by VIRGINIA WOOLF*

The passage follows the introductory paragraph where Mrs Ramsay has promised her son that they will go to the lighthouse if it is fine:

> 'But,' said his father, stopping in front of the drawing room window, 'it won't be fine'.
>
> Had there been an axe handy, a poker, or any weapon that would have gashed a hole in his father's breast and killed him, there and then, James would have seized it. Such were the extremes of emotion that Mr Ramsay excited in his children's breasts by his mere presence; standing, as now, lean as a knife, narrow as the blade of one, grinning sarcastically, not only with the pleasure of disillusioning his sons and casting ridicule upon his wife, who was ten thousand times better in every way than he was (James thought), but also with some secret conceit at his own accuracy of judgment. What he said was true. It was always true. He was incapable of untruth; never tampered with a fact; never altered a disagreeable word to suit the pleasure or convenience of any mortal being, least of all his own children who, sprung from his loins, should be aware from childhood that life is difficult; facts uncompromising; and the passage to that fabled land where our brightest hopes are extinguished, our frail barks founder in darkness (here Mr Ramsay would straighten his back and narrow his little blue eyes upon the horizon) one that needs, above all, courage, truth and the power to endure.

This is a passage where a small amount of descriptive narrative is interwoven in an extremely intricate manner with psychological analysis and it would be easy for the teacher to dictate a commentary to the effect that Virginia Woolf displays here an *introspective and impressionistic* style, well adapted to the description of the mental states of the characters. However, students would be liable to copy that verbatim into any future essay with only a vague sense of how Virginia Woolf achieves her effects.

They can be asked instead to perform a variety of very concrete tasks to find out how the passage works.

7.2.1 *Lexical features*

Get the students to look at word length and type by: (a) counting the number of words of three syllables or more; (b) working out how many words are abstract and how many concrete. They will find that the actual vocabulary used is not particularly difficult; only 13 words in the whole extract are of three syllables or more and only the Biblical and literary allusions in the expressions 'sprung from his loins' and 'our frail barks founder' are likely to be unknown to them. There are, however a high proportion of abstract words creating an impression of formality. The formality is increased by the proportionally greater use of nouns to adjectives, as in 'accuracy of judgment' instead of 'accurate judgment'.

7.2.2 Figurative language

Find the figures of speech in the extract and explore the connotations with the students. In the simile *lean as a blade and narrow as one* it is evident that *blade* hints at sharpness as well as narrowness and that *narrowness* can be mental as well as physical. The teacher can remind the students of the expressions 'narrow-minded' and 'sharp-tongued'.

Having explored all the Biblical and literary connotations of 'sprung from his loins' and 'our frail barks founder' ask the students why Virginia Woolf employs such language when describing Mr Ramsay. This should draw their attention to the way in which the language shapes our view of his character. Consider with them also the fact that truth is associated with unpleasantness in Mr Ramsay's life.

7.2.3 Internal structure

Here again set the students the positive task of counting: (a) the number of words in the sentences; (b) the number of finite verbs.

They can also try to find the connectors or meaning markers which indicate the structure of the paragraph.

One of the first things which will undoubtedly strike them is the great disparity in sentence length, ranging from 4 words to 95. The structure of the two long sentences, furthermore, is unusual and this is particularly true of the final sentence. It consists of little more than a rambling series of phrases and expressions linked by semi-colons and omits several finite verbs which one might have expected. This makes for considerable difficulty of comprehension, especially in the final clause which, due to the omission of 'is' appears to be incomplete.

The cohesion of the passage is not immediately apparent, although 'sprung from his loins' obviously correlates with children, and the image of Mr Ramsay narrowing his eyes upon the horizon conjures up the image of a sailor and so links with the 'frail barks' in the previous phrase. It is coherent, therefore, in that the ideas are related. The apparent lack of linguistic cohesion is due to two factors: the objective of the sentence alters half-way through, changing from narration to what is going on in Mr Ramsay's mind and the author has provided few guides to let us know that this is happening. Such a style is obviously adapted to convey the loosely connected, unhurrying impressions and sensations that flow through the mind.

7.2.4 *Tone*

Novels such as *To the Lighthouse* are often referred to as the 'stream of consciousness' genre, with James Joyce and Virginia Woolf as the most obvious exponents of the art. Such authors, rather than directly commenting on the events, appear to be trying to get inside the minds of their characters, to reproduce the internal flow of thoughts and impressions. The looseness of construction and the allusive vocabulary contribute to this impression. In the passage quoted Virginia Woolf is clearly trying to evoke our sympathy for Mrs Ramsay and James by revealing to us the rather cold blooded and uncompromising thoughts of Mr Ramsay. Since this internal flow is far less ordered and sequential than the descriptions of 'realistic' novelists it is referred to as impressionistic writing.

It should become evident as these lexical and structural features are examined that the distinctive character and appeal of Virginia Woolf's style lies in the ways in which she breaks or ignores common conventions; and students should be able to draw such conclusions from knowledge which they have derived themselves from the text.

7.3 Comparison and opposition

One technique which can be applied to most areas of stylistic analysis is that of comparison and opposition. It is very difficult to spotlight any particular stylistic trait in a vacuum. It must be seen in comparable or contrasting works and related to other writings. Parallel texts can therefore be used to exemplify the individual stylistic devices under consideration.

Different poems on the same subject are relatively easy to find; many secondary school text books are specifically designed in this way, setting poems on the same subject side by side so that students are aware of the different ways of approaching similar themes; e.g. *Touchstones* Vols 1, 2 and 3 by M G and P Benton (1970); *Reachout* Vols 1, 2 and 3 by Blackburn and Cunningham (1969).

Widdowson, in his book *Stylistics and the Teaching of Literature* (1975), showed how the description of a man in a passport, for a character reference and in a short story by Somerset Maugham, varied totally in approach, format and choice of salient features. Many modern adventure and spy stories capitalise on this fact by using apparently genuine police statements, supposed extracts from data files and official documents to convey maximum authenticity to the work (e.g. *Report to the Commissioner* by J Mills).

In order to provide examples of contrast the teacher can instruct the students to rewrite the passage under consideration themselves. Thus, in order to demonstrate the way in which the final sentence in the passage from *To the Lighthouse* is constructed the teacher might tell them to break it down into shorter sentences.

Sample rewritten passage

Mr Ramsay was incapable of untruth. He never tampered with a fact. He never altered a disagreeable word to suit the pleasure or convenience of any mortal being, least of all his own children. He frequently thought that they, who had sprung from his loins, should be aware that life is difficult. They should realise that facts are uncompromising. They should know that the passage to the fabled land where our brightest hopes are extinguished and our frail barks founder in darkness is one that needs, above all, courage, truth and the power to endure. Here Mr Ramsay would straighten his back and narrow his little blue eyes upon the horizon.

The students will discover that they have to insert *he frequently thought* half way through in order to effect the transfer from descriptive narrative to reported thoughts. And in order to include all of the original thoughts the penultimate sentence is still of considerable length and complexity.

The teacher might also oppose the work to that of another writer, the passages considered side by side so that the students are aware not only of the variation in length and complexity of the sentences, but even of the difference in rhythmic patterns when read aloud.

> Study the extract below taken from the beginning of *The Bridge of San Luis Rey*. It follows a description of the bridge and how it broke. Pay particular attention to:
> (a) sentence length
> (b) figurative language
> (c) tone.

Sample text from *The Bridge of San Luis Rey*

The bridge seemed to be among the things that last forever; it was unthinkable that it should break. The moment a Peruvian heard of the accident he signed himself and made a mental calculation as to how recently he had crossed by it and how soon he intended crossing by it again. People wandered about in a trance-like state, muttering: they had the hallucination of seeing themselves falling into a gulf.

There was a great service in the Cathedral. The bodies of the victims were approximately collected and approximately separated from one another, and there was a great searching of hearts in the beautiful city of Lima. Servant girls returned bracelets which they had stolen from their mistresses, and usurers harangued their wives angrily in defense of usury. Yet it was strange that this event should have so impressed the Limeans, for in that country those catastrophes which lawyers shockingly call the 'Acts of God' were more than usually frequent. Tidal waves were continually washing away cities; earthquakes arrived every week and towers fell upon good men and women all the time. Diseases were for ever flitting in and out of the provinces, and old age carried away some of the most admirable citizens. That is why it was so surprising that the Peruvians should have been especially touched by the rent in the bridge of San Luis Rey.

Both this passage and the one from *To the Lighthouse* are designed to introduce the reader to the main themes of their respective stories but are obviously very different in tone and style. The sentences in the Thornton Wilder passage are for a start much shorter. Where sentences are slightly longer they are neatly balanced, the second half paralleling the first.

People wandered about in a trance-like state, muttering: they had the hallucination of seeing themselves falling into a gulf.

This is a parallelism where *trance-like state* balances with *hallucination*. Of the 10 sentences in the extract 7 contain only between 18–25 words and of the remaining 3 the longest has 34, reflecting a much more even distribution of sentence length than that in the passage from *To the Lighthouse*. The students should perceive that these shorter sentences make for a pithy, aphoristic style and lend themselves admirably to the slightly humorous approach that Wilder has taken to the disaster. He makes much use of irony and exaggeration ('Tidal waves were continually washing away cities; earthquakes arrived every week') seeming to assure his readers that they are not to take all of this too seriously. James' hatred of Mr Ramsay, on the other hand, is, we feel, only too genuine, as is Mr Ramsay's joyless attitude to life.

7.4 Discourse situation and purpose

It is plain that the authors' relationship to the reader is very different in the two books. While Virginia Woolf appears to be trying to efface herself from the narrative so that we have the impression of actually being inside the minds of Mr Ramsay and James, Wilder as narrator is intruding on the story, trying to direct our attention in this way or that.

The theme of *The Bridge of San Luis Rey* is that of divine intervention, or the lack of it, and Wilder wishes to question whether God was, in fact, responsible for the deaths of the five who fall from the bridge, and whether the event revealed a latent pattern in human life. He could just have told the story and allowed his readers to draw their own conclusions. He chooses, instead, to introduce Brother Juniper, a small Franciscan friar who observes the accident, sees the five gesticulating figures thrown into the valley below and resolves to inquire into the disaster:

> Anyone else would have said to himself with secret joy: 'Within ten minutes myself . . .' But it was another thought that visited Brother Juniper: 'Why did this happen to *those* five?' If there were any plan in the universe at all, if there were any pattern in human life, surely it could be discovered mysteriously latent in those lives so suddenly cut off. Either we live by accident and die by accident, or we live by plan and die by plan. And on that instant Brother Juniper made the resolve to inquire into the secret lives of those five persons that moment falling through the air, and to surprise the reason for their taking off.

Wilder, furthermore, is not content with having one person comment on the action, but also comments himself as the narrator, laughing gently at Brother Juniper's ideas and putting forward his own.

Although this might all seem rather complicated it can easily be seen that it has the effect of bringing the readers into collusion with the author and encouraging them to speculate themselves on the main theme. The dual approach means that we are given both sides of the argument, Brother Juniper's and the narrator's.

Students can be asked to identify the author's purpose in introducing Brother Juniper and, once again, can be given selected passages to reread in groups along with sets of leading questions.

Sample questions
1 Why is the first chapter entitled 'Perhaps an accident'?
2 Who is Brother Juniper and why does he write his book?
3 Why are we told about the master of San Martin University?
4 What does Brother Juniper conclude about the deaths?
5 Why is Brother Juniper put to death?
6 Does any good come out of the accident?
7 What are the narrator's conclusions?

Students should be able to see that the story has been used as a vehicle for the narrator's ideas about divine intervention in a very overt manner. In *To the Lighthouse*, on the other hand, there is no 'I' persona, no overt narrator and the approach seems to make for great psychological realism.

7.5 Comic works

The question of authorial attitude is also very important when considering comic works. Issues and characters are frequently presented in a totally different way to those in realistic works and students cannot be expected to respond to and evaluate such texts in the same way as realistic ones.

They need to realise that the comic author is not aiming at a sympathetic insight into reality, but is presenting a detached, perhaps mocking view of the human situation. Affectations, foibles and idiosyncracies are liable to be emphasized. The author may concentrate on or exaggerate one quality to the exclusion of others, sometimes to the point where a character becomes a caricature, like Jonson's Volpone. The style may, therefore, be obtrusive and the reader obliged to pay more than the usual attention to the method and manner of narration. Much use may be made of incongruity and contrast; the laws of syntax, punctuation or spelling may be suspended. The appeal often lies in the inventive and imaginative handling of the language, rather than a comprehensive overview of human experience.

Provide the students, therefore, with examples of the types of language most used by comic writers, the figures of irony and paradox, understatement and exaggeration. Irony, for example, is used to convey meaning by words whose literal significance is the opposite of what is intended. When Jerome K Jerome says:

I like work: it fascinates me. I can sit and look at it for hours.

it is obvious that, in fact, he does *not* like work.

Students can be given a series of quotations similar to this to analyse so that when they are faced with Mark Antony's funeral oration in Julius Caesar they will be prepared for the fact that when Antony says *honourable* he means *dishonourable*.

Help them to see also the humorous possibilities in breaks or sudden changes in register.

> What is comical about Brother Juniper resolving to enquire into the reasons for the five's *taking off*? What did he mean?

It should also be borne in mind that while situation and characters may be quite unrealistic this does not mean that the comic writer has nothing serious to say, merely that he attacks human failings from a different angle. Although Wilder intends us to laugh at Brother Juniper he also uses him to illustrate the evils perpetrated by the Church at that time by having him burnt at the stake at the end.

Dickens, with all his delight in language, still managed to make plain some of the disturbing aspects of the society of his day. Some of his characters (e.g. Fagin in *Oliver Twist*) are comic in some respects but are also truly evil. The students can be encouraged, therefore, to approach such works in the same way as they would realistic ones, i.e. identify the social and personal themes, get some idea of the characters and work out the writer's distinctive tactics.

Remember that humour is one of the most difficult qualities to transfer since it depends, perhaps more than others, upon common cultural assumptions. Jane Austen, for example, is one of the most realistic of the comic novelists, her humour lying in her exact capturing of human weaknesses and expressing them with elegance, but the ability to find her novels funny depends to a large extent on a good understanding of the society in which they are based.

In conclusion, it should be noted that although the areas of content and form have been covered separately they will both need to be taken into account when preparing a text for a class. There is always considerable overlap and some texts lend themselves more to a discussion of style than others. Once again, however, it must be stressed that students should be able to cope with this level of criticism and that it should be used to heighten their enjoyment and appreciation of the works they read and not just as an academic exercise.

8 Figurative language and poetry

It is commonly assumed that figurative language will be too difficult for foreign learners to cope with and that therefore poetry and highly figurative texts will be out of their reach. A British *Schools Council Report* said, for example:

> For many second language learners, especially those first exposed to English at a late stage of their schooling, and for all pupils whose linguistic and cultural experience may be limited, it is pedagogically expedient to defer detailed consideration of figurative language and to introduce very gradually works embodying some of the conventions, styles and imagery of imaginative writing (Fallows 1983).

However, while it is true in some instances that figurative language is beyond the scope of foreign learners it is not true in all. Some short poems and figurative works can safely be included early on, especially translations of the local literature to minimise the problem of cultural displacement. The teacher will, however, need to weigh carefully what sort of understanding is called for in such readings.

Metaphorical language has been defined as everyday things in unusual juxtaposition, or the comparison of dissimilars. Much of our everyday idiom is 'frozen' metaphor, metaphor which was once new and vivid but has now become so well used as to pass unnoticed (eg *put your foot down, lose your head*). When used by a great writer, metaphorical language will cause the reader to see some object or event in a new light, and providing that the language is not of itself strange, the metaphor should be as easy to understand for a foreign learner as it is for a native speaker. When Aquino says in *The Honorary Consul* by Graham Greene that 'poetry drops like an eagle and stabs before you know' both the EFL learner and the English reader can recognise the jolt of emotion which an unexpected line in a poem can give, just like the eagle's pounce on some small animal.

Initially, consideration of figurative language will be of a fairly simplistic nature but as time goes on and the students develop in their ability to respond to texts in a more sophisticated way, they will be able to study figurative works in more detail. They can be given examples of the most important figures of speech and help to understand the ways in which they are used by writers to create their effects. Such language might be related to:

- imagery—simile and metaphor (including personification and symbolism) synecdoche and metonymy
- tone–including understatement and hyperbole, register shift and irony and, in case of poetry particularly:
- sound devices—rhyme, alliteration (including assonance and consonance) and onomatopoeia.

(See the Glossary for examples of most of the above figures of speech.)

8.1 Understanding figurative language

All metaphorical language depends upon a comparison of some sort, whether introduced by *like* or *as* (as in a simile) or actually identifying one thing with another. Thus, when Carl Sandburg says:

The fog comes on little cat feet

it conjures up a brief picture in the mind, an image of the fog drifting with the smooth, liquid movement and quietness of a cat.

Students need to acquire the ability to speculate about an author's intentions when he uses figurative language, and the connotations and allusions contained in the figures should be explored in depth. It is not sufficient, for example, to say that Rossetti's *My heart is like a singing bird* is a simile; the various associations between song birds and happiness need to be considered with the students. A variety of exercises can be used to assist them:

Exercise A
Place the metaphor and its everyday equivalent side by side and allow the students to say why they think the metaphor is the more revealing.

1 the great, gold ball of day
   sprang up from the dark hill
   The sun rose above the hill (Judith Wright)
2 And how the silence surged softly backwards
   When the plunging hooves were gone
   It was silent again after he rode off (Walter de la Mare)

Exercise B
Supply a choice of words or phrases to replace those which bear the metaphoric weight of the extract and allow the students to choose which they find the most effective.

1   How the silence (flowed, slithered, surged, streamed) back
    When the (plunging, clattering, noisy, clip-clopping) hooves were gone.
2   Her eyes, lost in the fatty ridge of her face, looked like:
    a) two small pieces of coal pressed into a lump of dough
    b) two raisins in a lump of dough
    c) two black buttons on a white lumpy cushion

from A Rose for Emily by W Faulkner

Exercise C
Prepare students for an effective metaphor by asking them to produce their own description of the object or event before reading the passage. Asking them to describe snow falling on a town, for example, could be a prelude to reading *London Snow* by Robert Bridges or *First Snow in Alsace* by Richard Wilbur.

8.1.1 *Tone*

The tone of a piece of writing depends largely on the writer's attitude to his or her work, whether he or she intends to be taken literally or whether he or she is using certain figures of speech such as hyperbole (exaggeration) to evoke a particular state of mind in his or her reader. Hyperbole can, for example, reflect the stress of great emotion as when Lady Macbeth in *Macbeth*, after the murder of Duncan says:

> Here's the smell of blood still. All the perfumes
> Of Arabia will not sweeten this little hand

or it can be used for the sake of emphasis or humour.

Tone is not always stable; it can shift between the tragic and comic, between the elevated and the mundane. This is often accomplished by what is referred to as *register shift*, a rapid change in diction, usually moving between high-flown literary language and ordinary speech. Henry Reed used register shift poetically in his *The Naming of Parts*:

> Today we have naming of parts. Yesterday
> We had daily cleaning. And tomorrow morning
> We shall have what to do after firing. But today
> Today we have naming of parts. Japonica
> Glistens like coral in all the neighbouring gardens
> And today we have naming of parts.

In this stanza and in each of the four succeeding ones formalised military jargon is opposed to poetic imagery (the japonica glistening like coral), the difference highlighting the contrast between the commonplace lesson in rifle assembly and the setting of the beautiful but indifferent natural world. Students can classify the two sorts of language in the poem and can even, in very advanced classes, attempt a stanza of their own.

Much modern poetry depends for its effect on strange collocations or a mixture of registers (e.g. Auden's *The Unknown Citizen*) and a variety of exercises for helping students to be aware of these aspects of language were suggested in Chapter 5. Further reading on the subject may be found in Carter and Burton (1982).

8.1.2 *Allusion*

Although, by and large, figurative language is accessible to all students, providing the actual lexis and structure are plain and the language is not highly idiomatic, there is the area of allusion which is rather more difficult for foreign learners.

Allusion is figurative language that relies on the rich background of English literature to make its point, the embedded quotation, the half-hidden reference to somebody else's metaphorical language. These are quotations which are altered a little and assimilated into the prose or poem without quotation marks, and it is difficult to understand the text without being familiar with the source of the allusion. T S Eliot, for example makes much use of allusive quotation in *The Waste Land* and part of the poem contains the lines:

When lovely woman stoops to folly and
Paces about her room again alone,
She smoothes her hair with automatic hand
And puts a record on the gramophone

The line *When lovely woman stoops to folly* is taken straight from Oliver Goldsmith's *The Vicar of Wakefield*; and it is obviously necessary to know that in Goldsmith's poem the *lovely woman* has to die to redeem herself to appreciate the irony of Eliot's lovely lady merely smoothing her hair and putting on a record.

It is true that Eliot records the classical and literary sources used in *The Waste Land* in notes accompanying the poem but one's appreciation or understanding of a poem is infinitely better if one does not need to be told constantly who or what is being referred to. A poem which needs almost total annotation is no longer a poem, but merely another comprehension exercise.

Having said this, however, it is clear that there is no such thing as literary knowledge which is common to all people and certainly some poetry is worth the trouble of familiarising oneself with the background. Certain works will appear in examinations and a degree of background knowledge will help students in their general reading. They can be assisted in this task by the teacher's:

- choosing carefully the edition: some are annotated with the foreign learner in mind
- providing some Easy Readers which contain information liable to be useful in poetry reading (e.g. Retold Greek Tales)
- devoting some classes to classical background, culture, etc.
- providing a crib to some of the allusion.

Real appreciation of allusion comes eventually with an ever-increasing knowledge of the literature and, as in Bright and McGregor's virtuous circle, the more one reads the more one recognises.

8.2 The poetry lesson

Figurative language is liable to appear more frequently and more overtly in poetic works and is therefore liable to receive more attention in the poetry lesson than elsewhere. As with novels and plays, poetry may be approached through the twin channels of content and form.

Two of the major differences between poetry and prose are those of rhyme and metre and students should be helped to get to know the various sound devices used by the poets. These can include

- rhyme (including internal rhyme)
- alliteration (including assonance and consonance)
- onomatopoeia, in which words are formed in imitation of the sound referred to (e.g. ducks *quack*, bells *tinkle*).

There is also the question of rhythm. While it is not usually necessary to burden the students with all the technical jargon for stress schemes (e.g. iambic and trochaic metres) they should be helped to develop a feeling for the different rhythms of poetry. It is often difficult for foreign students to 'hear' mentally the rhythms of a poem, the cadences, the sheer sound of the words when they read it to themselves. Correct intonation and stress are usually the most difficult aspects of a foreign language to acquire and inadequacy in those areas can confuse understanding far more than mispronunciation. It is therefore important that the poem is read to them, either by the teacher or by a professional actor on a recording.

There are many professional recordings of poetry (Argo recordings being one of the most prestigious), although care does need to be taken in the choice of reader. Some authors are ill served by their own recordings. Clarity is important as is the emotional appeal of the work.

Having played or read the poem to the class a couple of times it is sometimes possible to let the students 'read along' with the teacher. This is especially effective with strongly rhythmic pieces since the students will be able to feel for themselves the beat of the metre. *Hiawatha*, for example, has been powerfully dramatised by the National Youth Theatre, a rousing production with much ululation and chanting (which contrasts splendidly with the haunting lyricism of Old Nokomis's lullaby) and this would form a very good accompaniment to a class 'chant along'.

Classroom presentation can also be varied by playing students the musical version of some poetry. John Betjeman has recorded some of his poems to the music of Jim Parker. T S Eliot's *Old Possum's Book of Practical Cats* has been turned into a musical play *Cats* with music by Andrew Lloyd Webber and has the virtue of some exciting tunes as well as being very faithful to the original text.

Such recorded versions of poems, however, need to be carefully prepared and presented and the sample texts and lesson plan which follow address this problem. It must be stressed that there is no one single approach to poetry presentation and each teacher has his own style. Two main principles, however, stand out:

1 It is usually better to let the students *hear* the poem before they see the text;
2 Work on figurative language should try to draw on the students' own store of associations.

Sample text 1 *The Griesly Wife* by John Manifold

If the students are going to hear the text first it may be necessary to supply some of the vocabulary in advance: certain expressions, for example, which are unknown to them and which are essential to an understanding of the poem, or references to other works (such as the Bible) which they might not be familiar with. This should ensure that the poem can make an impact at its first reading.

In the poem *The Griesly Wife* a young newly married woman, living in the Australian outback, suddenly leaves her house in the middle of the night and goes out barefoot into the snow. Her husband follows the tracks of the two bare feet, at first angry that she should have played such a trick on him and then, suddenly, badly frightened as he realises that the two foot track has ended and that a four foot track leads on—a track, says the poem, that is 'never of human feet'. It concludes:

> At first he started walking back
> And then began to run
> And his quarry wheeled at the end of her track
> And hunted him, in turn.

> O long the fire may burn for him
> And open stand the door
> And long the bed may wait, empty
> He'll not be back, any more.

The language of the poem is relatively simple apart from a small amount of local vocabulary (e.g. *gum-wood* fire and *dingoes*) but the key words are *quarry* and *wheeled*. If the students do not understand those two words the whole impact of the poem is lost. Although part of the charm of verse is the sense of mystery provoked by half-understood phrases the key words must be understood, nevertheless, and in this poem the key lies in those two words. There is therefore a good case for eliciting such vocabulary in advance, perhaps even at a previous lesson.

Sample text 2 *Piazza piece* by John Crowe Ransome

> I am a gentleman in a dustcoat trying
> To make you hear. Your ears are soft and small
> And listen to an old man not at all,
> They want the young men's whispering and sighting.
> But see the roses on your trellis dying
> And hear the spectral singing of the moon;
> For I must have my lovely lady soon
> I am a gentleman in a dustcoat trying

> —I am a lady young in beauty waiting
> Until my true love comes, and then we kiss.
> But what grey man among the vines is this
> Whose words are dry and faint as in a dream?
> Back from my trellis, sir, before I scream!
> I am a lady young in beauty waiting.

Sample approach

AIM: To assist students to see that this is an ironically presented miniature drama, that the old gentleman is not just an unwanted suitor but Death and the poem is a variation of the allegory of Death and the Maiden.

PREPARATION: If possible, record the poem, preferably with a colleague of the opposite sex. Ideally a very thin, dry, old man's voice is needed for the Gentleman and a high, innocent, young girl's voice for the Lady. Obtain also a recording of a minuet, if possible. Plan the questions to be asked before or after each reading.

MATERIALS: A tape-recorder, dictionary, book of quotations.

PRESENTATIONS: See lesson plan, pages 104-105.

The lesson plan shows how students can be gradually introduced to the text and can be led by various 'clues' to work out what the poem is trying to say. In this case the sonnet, with the regularity of an old-fashioned minuet, presents the image of Death as a dry-as-dust old man, anxious to get the young lady into his clutches. In formal and pedantic language it hints not only at the inevitability but also the formality of death. Form and content thus work together to produce an extraordinary and unique work, the form illuminating the content in a way that a different method of structuring material would not have done.

In this chapter a variety of methods of presenting figurative works have been explored. It must not be forgotten, however, that the point of any exercise on a set text, whether related to imagery, register study or form, is that it should add to the students' enjoyment of the text. It should not just be 'useful' language, even though we may be considering literature as an integral part of our language study. Rather such studies should enable students to catch the full richness and flavour of the text and encourage them to come back for more.

SAMPLE LESSON PLAN *Piazza Piece* by John Crowe Ransome

Steps	Aims	Preparation & Notes	Students
1 *Play the tape through once and ask simple questions*	to give them a simplified over-all view of the work	Set simple factual questions or those requiring yes/no answers ● Which two people are speaking? ● Is the young lady interested in the old gentleman?	Listen and Reply to questions
2 *Hand out some more questions and play the tape a second time*	to establish the meaning of some of the unknown vocabulary (*piazza, trellis, dustcoat, spectre*) the questions given in advance will give them something specific to listen for during the second reading.	The questions given in advance moving from the factual to the more evaluative. ● Where is the young lady sitting? (The fact that Ransome is American is relevant since *piazza* was the name given to the verandah in the American South) ● What is the man wearing? ● How does the moon sing? ● What sort of vines are they? ● Do you think her love will come?	Listen, Discuss answers in pairs Reply
3 *Explain associations with Victorian melodrama*	to help students to understand the allusion in *Back from my trellis, sir, before I scream* to wicked Sir Jasper in melodrama. to help them see the irony in the poem	A short sample of a Victorian melodrama	Suggest similar works in their own culture
4 *Play the association game*	to assist students to see the connotations of the key words used in the poem (*roses, spectral dust*)	Teacher's list *Roses*: beauty, my love is like a red red rose, perfume, roses in her cheeks *Spectre*: ghosts, chains pale shapes graveyards, the dead *Dust*: dirt, dryness, ashes to ashes dust to dust, dustbin, the way to dusty death	Draw up lists of words readily associated with the key words Work in groups One to be assigned to look up words in book of quotations

		Prepare multiple-choice lists	Suggest own associations
5 Distribute the text and review the students' associations nb It might be necessary to choose a different local flower if the rose is totally unknown but choose one which has the same connotations	to help students realise the themes of Youth and Health associated with the Lady (roses in her cheeks, the bloom of health, the bloom of youth) and of Death with the Gentleman (ashes to ashes, dust to dust, the grey man)	a gentleman in a [raincoat / trenchcoat / greatcoat / overcoat] the [cheerful / tuneful / morbid] singing of the moon [ghostly]	Suggest own associations
6 Play the tape a third time Suggest they listen particularly to the sound of the verse Play also the minuet	to draw their attention to the rhymes dying, trying, sighing and show how they contribute to the effect by the mournful fading away at the line endings alliterated hissing noise in old man's speech		Listen Practice reading mournfully with a friend!
7 With more advanced students Consider the form of the poem	to help students to see that the formality of the sonnet form contributes directly to the effect created by the poem, as do the formal titles 'sir' and 'lady'. to assist students to recognise the irony implicit in the form sonnets being originally devoted to love poetry whereas the poem is really about death	Teacher information Petrarchan sonnet (14 lines 8 & 6) Gentleman eight-line stanza/octave Lady six-line stanza/sestet Rhyme scheme: abbaaccaa addeea Lines 1 and 8,9 and 14 are repeated. Mention the demureness of the young lady, sitting waiting for her true love 'and then we kiss'. Stress the formality of the situation	Students to identify the form, work out the rhyme scheme and stanza form, and identify formal terms in the poem
8 Explain the allegory Death and the Maiden			
9 Have them discuss the poem in groups	Is this poem really a repetition of the allegory Death and the Maiden? In what other ways has death been represented? Would the poem work as a play or film?		
Evaluate			

10 Summary

The scope of this book has been to show that a study of literature and a study of language can be mutually supportive, that a literature study can contribute to the students' command of the language generally as well as to their personal, social and moral development. The aim has been to demonstrate how the students themselves (with a guiding hand from the teacher) can get the most out of the materials such methods might involve:

Breaking it down
Students are encouraged to abstract from the material
(a) themes
(b) characters
(c) the framework of the text

Reforming it
Students encouraged to make the work their own by

Writing
(a) making linear notes (e.g. story or character indexes)
(b) constructing diagrams, flow-charts, maps etc
(c) rewriting the story
   • from a different character's point of view
   • from a neutral observer's point of view
   • in a different format (e.g. as a newspaper report of the event or a script for play or film)
(d) making a summary of a section or chapter.

Orally
(a) retelling the story—either in the story game or to a partner or small group (perhaps with the support of notes)
(b) taking part in a role play simulation working from assignment cards containing the role, situation and strategies. Simulations can be
   • episodes from the book (with or without dialogue supplied)
   • imaginary episodes (whether referred to in the text or not)
   • television/radio interviews with characters from the book.

Comparing and contrasting it

Students to compare/contrast the text with extra material which may be

(a) on similar themes
(b) in similar settings
(c) in a contrasting style

Such extra material might be

- Graded Readers
- extracts from other works
- a film of the work.

Completing it

Students to replace parts of the text which the teacher has deleted. Deletions can be

(a) single words, deleted on a regular numerical basis, usually between five and seven word intervals (a cloze test)
(b) single words deleted on an irregular basis to highlight certain stylistic techniques or vocabulary.
(c) idiomatic phrases.

Rearranging it

Students to reorder parts put into random order. These can be

- whole story sequences
- sections of a chapter
- individual sentences.

Making predictions about it

(a) endings to individual sections
(b) endings to the story as a whole
(c) events occurring after the conclusion of the story.

Playing games based on it

Students to use the work as the basis for a variety of games e.g. Call My Bluff, Twenty Questions, The Story Game etc.

Discussing it

Finally, and most importantly, the students should be encouraged to discuss the material, discussions relating to Character, Theme, Moral Questions etc. They can be helped with assignment cards which contain:

(a) a set of leading questions
    OR a series of statements representing a range of views

(b) a set of strategies for conducting the discussion

(c) references to where they can find the information.

They can be encouraged to set their own questions on the subject or read a passage of their own choosing relating to their theme.

Literature can therefore provide students with language in action, a living context and focal point for them in their own efforts to communicate. It will help them develop a variety of language skills such as the prediction or inference of meaning from the linguistic or situational context, or, perhaps, the ability to detect an author's intentions from the 'tone' markers. As they relate their reading to their own knowledge of the world and experience they will internalise the structures and lexis to the point where language recognition becomes automatic and the material will become a stimulus to their own language production.

Literature study is obviously linked to language study but it is to be hoped that students will acquire more thereby than just a knowledge of the language. Literature, carefully chosen, can open up and enrich the language lesson, provide students with a window on new worlds and engage their intellect and emotions in a way that study of the language alone can not.

The role of the teacher in this enrichment is an intricate one. It is, in effect, a balancing act between explaining how the language is made up and making plain what it is trying to say. A lot must therefore be left to the teacher's intuition as to how much information, help and advice the students will need; but assuming the right balance is found students can hope to derive both pleasure and profit, wisdom and delight from their study of literature.

Appendix A

Texts set for the University of Cambridge Examinations in English as a Foreign Language, 1985, 1986 and 1987.

I FIRST CERTIFICATE IN ENGLISH

J B Priestley, *An Inspector Calls*
George Orwell, *Animal Farm*
George Bernard Shaw, *Arms and the Man*
Longmans Simplified English, *Outstanding Short Stories*
Peter Dickinson, *The Seventh Raven*
M Swan (Ed.), *Zero Hour*

II CERTIFICATE OF PROFICIENCY IN ENGLISH

George Eliot, *Silas Marner*
Robert Graves, *Goodbye to all That*
Margaret Drabble, *The Millstone*
Patricia Highsmith, *The Talented Mr Ripley*
John Arden, *Serjeant Musgrave's Dance*
John Osborne, *The Entertainer*
D H Lawrence, *Selected Tales*

OPTIONAL ADDITIONAL PAPER
Dickens, *Great Expectations*
Shakespeare, *Julius Caesar*, *Twelfth Night*
Wordsworth, *The Prelude*, Books 1 and 2
Gaskell, *North and South*
Forster, *A Room with a View*
Graham Greene, *The Quiet American*, *Dr Fischer of Geneva*
Edna O'Brian, *Mrs Reinhardt and other stories*
John Fowles, *The Collector*
Doris Lessing, *The Grass is Singing*
John Betjeman, *The Best of Betjeman*

III DIPLOMA OF ENGLISH STUDIES

Literature A

1 Shakespeare, *Antony and Cleopatra*, *Coriolanus*, *Measure for Measure*, *The Sonnets*, *Love's Labours Lost*, *Richard II*
2 Marlowe, Donne, Sheridan, Boswell (*Life of Johnson*), Milton (*Comus and shorter poems*), Swift

Literature B

1 Coleridge, Blake, Byron (*Don Juan*), Cobbett (*Rural Rides*), Scott W, Jane Austen (any two novels)
2 Dickens (*Dombey and Son*), Wright (Ed.) (*Seven Victorian Poets*), Tennyson, Charlotte Brontë, Prose extracts in *Victorian Prose and poetry* (Oxford Anthology)

Literature C

1 Henry James (*The Turn of the Screw*), James Joyce, H G Wells, Ezra Pound, Virginia Woolf, *The Faber Book of Modern Verse*
2 Jean Rhys, Basil Bunting (*Collected Poems*), Patrick White, V S Naipaul, Donald Davie, Allan Bennett, Philip Larkin

Appendix B
Anthologies of extracts from literature and original short stories

Upper intermediate or advanced students

Reading Between the Lines, John McRae and Roy Boardman, Cambridge University Press, 1984
An anthology of English poetry and prose organised thematically (e.g. Family, War, Women) with exercises on both content and style

Language for Literature, Richard Walker, Collins, 1983
A selection of modern English prose with language and content exercises

Twentieth Century English Short Stories (Eds.) Tina Pierce and Edward Cochrane, Bell and Hyman, 1984
An anthology of short stories with notes and exercises

Advanced students

A Day Saved and other modern stories (Ed.) Peter Taylor, 1979

Samphire and other modern stories (Ed.) Michael Swan, 1977

Poem to Poem: Reading and writing poems with students of English, Alan Maley and Sandra Moulding, Cambridge University Press, 1985

A Roald Dahl Selection, Roy Blatchford, Longman
A selection of Dahl's short stories with points for discussion

Appendix C

Audio-visual aids

Audio-Cassettes and Video Cassettes

Types of Cassette

1 General Introduction e.g. *An Introduction to Commonwealth Literature* (2), *The Novel since 1950* (2)
2 Individual writers, e.g. Achebe (2)
3 Dramatisation and extracts of works e.g. Greene's *The Third Man* (5)
4 Criticism of specific texts, e.g. Arden: *Serjeant Musgrave's Dance*, (5) Orwell: *Nineteen Eighty Four* (5), Dickens: *Great Expectations* (8)
5 Audio cassette with accompanying slides/filmstrips e.g. *How to Read and Understand Drama* (7)
6 Poetry: Individual writers, e.g. Stevie Smith (1)
        Anthologies: e.g. *Six centuries of Verse* (6)
7 Complete versions of texts: e.g. *Jane Eyre* (3)

Producers/Distributors—Audio-cassettes

1 ARGO: 15 St George Street, London W1R 9DE
2 THE BRITISH COUNCIL: 65 Davies Street, London W1Y 2AA
3 COVER TO COVER CASSETTES: Dene House, Lockeridge, Marlborough, Wilts
4 EXETER TAPES: St Fagans Road, Fairwater, Cardiff CF5 3AE
5 TALKTAPES: 13 Croftdown Road, London NW5 1EL
6 THAMES TELEVISION INTERNATIONAL: 149 Tottenham Court Rd, London W1P 9LL
7 EDUCATIONAL AUDIO-VISUAL Mary Glasgow Publications, Brookehampton Lane, Kineton, Warwick CV35 0JB
8 AUDIO LEARNING, Unit 1, The Works, 105A Torriano Avenue, London NW5 2RX

Producers/Distributors—Video-cassettes

1 THE BRITISH COUNCIL: as above
2 PENGUIN STUDY VIDEO
3 BBC EXTERNAL BUSINESS AND DEVELOPMENT GROUP PO Box 76, Bush House, London, WC2B 4PH
4 THAMES TELEVISION INTERNATIONAL: as above

Appendix D

Textgrader
Disk for RML 308Z, disk and cassette for BBC Micro
Hutchinson Publishing Group, 17-21 Conway Street, London W1.

Textgrader provides automatic estimates of the difficulty of a text on the basis of any of seven systems—Mugford, Fry, Flesch, Smog, Fog, FORCAST or the FJP index.

The user needs only to load the program, type in a sample of text, and read the score. The normal sample for these indices is 100 words, and the computer will either give a score for one or calculate an average result for up to seven samples. It also counts the hundred words.

Glossary

Alliteration: the repetition of consonants at the start of consecutive or near consecutive words
e.g. Five *miles meandering with a mazy motion*

Archaism: language no longer in use: e.g. *hearken* for *listen*

Assonance: repetition of identical or similar vowels, usually applied to sounds in the middle of words
e.g. So *twice five miles of fertile ground*

Cohesion: the linguistic means by which various parts of a text are related to each other and to the work as a whole

Collocation: two or more words which are often associated together
e.g. *cheque book* or *bank statement*

Coherence: the underlying thoughts and ideas which relate various parts of a text to each other

Communicative function: the way in which language is *used* to communicate
e.g. make an apology, ask for information

Compound words a word composed of two original words e.g. *blackbird, windmill, heartbeat*

Connotation: the area of association, suggestion and implication which surround a certain word e.g. *Fragrance* has pleasant connotations, *stink* unpleasant although they both mean *smell*

Consonance: the repetition of identical or similar consonants, usually in the middle of words
e.g. Blue, glossy green and velvet black
They coiled and swam; and every track (*Coleridge*)

Diction: the manner of expression of language whether spoken (e.g. clear or muffled) or written (e.g. literary or colloquial)

Extensive reading: the relatively rapid reading of longer texts

Hyperbole: exaggeration for emphasis or humour or under the stress of great emotion

	e.g. earthquakes arrived every week and towers fell upon good men and women all the time
Idiom:	phrases and expressions which have a meaning different to that of the individual parts
	e.g. *under the weather* (feel slightly ill)
Intensive reading:	the relatively slower reading of short extracts along with close consideration of syntax and lexis
Irony:	the suggesting of one meaning by stating the opposite
	e.g. It is justifiable to enter into war against our nearest ally if one of his town lies convenient for us.
	(It is totally unjustifiable) (*Swift*)
Metaphor:	a comparison made between two essentially unlike things by identifying one with the other
	e.g. The burnt out ends of smoky days (*T S Eliot*)
Metonymy:	in which the name of one thing is put for another with which it is usually associated. Symbolism is a form of metonymy
	e.g. The pen is mightier than the sword
Onomatopoeia:	words formed or arranged in imitation of a sound
	e.g. hens *cluck*, ducks *quack*
Paradox:	two seemingly contradictory statements joined together to express a truth e.g. There are two tragedies in life. One is not to get your heart's desire; the other is to get it (*G B Shaw*)
Personification:	a specific kind of metaphor where personality and life are ascribed to inanimate or abstract objects
	e.g. Daybreak struggled with the gloom under the arcades of the Plaza (*Conrad*)
Register:	in a general sense, the different varieties of English related to the topic of discussion; the use of the language (e.g. religious, legal language)
Regression:	a backward movement of the eye in reading to cover material already looked at
Simile:	an explicit comparison introduced by *like*, *as* or *than*
	e.g. My heart is like an apple tree
	Whose boughs are bent with thick-set fruit (*Rossetti*)
Sonnet:	verse containing fourteen ten-syllable lines, rhymed according to one of several schemes (e.g. Petrarchan)
Synecdoche:	in which the whole is used for a part or a part for a whole
	e.g. I should have been a pair of ragged claws

Scuttling across the floor of silent seas (a crab) (*T S Eliot*)

Understatement: saying less than one means, usually with ironic intent e.g. Mr Knightley seemed to be trying not to smile and <u>succeeded without difficul</u>ty upon Mrs Elton's beginning to talk to him (*J Austen*)

Bibliography

Bright, J A and McGregor, G P, *Teaching English as a Second Language*, London: Longman, 1970

Brumfit, C J (ed) *Teaching Literature Overseas: Language-Based Approaches*, ELT Documents 115, Oxford: Pergamon Press, 1983

Cairns, H S and Cairns, C E, *Psycholinguistics: A Cognitive View of Language*, New York: Holt Rinehart and Winston, 1976

Carey, J, 'Visiting India' in *The Sunday Times* 6 July, 1983

Carter, R and Burton, D (eds) *Literary Text and Language Study*, London: Edward Arnold, 1982

Enkvist, N E, Spencer, J and Gregory, M, *Linguistics and Style*, London: Oxford University Press, 1964

Fallows, L, *Assessment in a multi-cultural society: English at 16* for Schools Council, York: Longman, 1983

Fowler, W S, 'Literature for Adult Students of English as a Foreign Language' in *English Language Teaching Journal* XXVI 1 Oct 1971

Fry, E, 'Fry's Readability Graph' in *Journal of Reading* No 20, 1977

Gilroy-Scott, N, 'Introduction' in Brumfit, C J (1983), *op. cit.*

Harrison, C, *Readability in the Classroom*, Cambridge: Cambridge Educational, 1980

Hedge, T, *Using Readers in the Language Classroom*, London: Macmillan, 1985

Hindmarsh, R, *Passing in Literature*, London: Cambridge University Press, 1972

Horner, S, *Best Laid Plans: English Teachers at Work* for Schools Council, York: Longman, 1983

Krashen, S D, *The Input Hypothesis*, Harlow: Longman, 1985

Leech, G N and Short, M, *Style in Fiction*, London: Longman, 1981

Lindsay, P H and Norman, D A, *Human Information Processing*, 2nd Edition, New York: Academic Press, 1977

McGregor, G P, *English in Africa*, Unesco: Heinemann, 1971

Mosback, G and Mosback, V, *Practical Faster Reading*, Cambridge: Cambridge University Press, 1976

Reeves, N, 'The uses of literature' in *The Linguist* Vol 25, No 1, 1986

Revell, J, *Teaching Techniques for Communicative English*, London: Macmillan, 1979

Riding, R J, *School Learning: Mechanisms and Processes*, London: Open Books, 1977

Rodger, A, 'Language for Literature' in Brumfit, C J (1983), *op. cit.*

Rodway, A, *The Craft of Criticism*, Cambridge: Cambridge University Press, 1982

Rudzka, B, Channell, J, Putseys, Y, Ostyn, P, *The Words You Need*, London: Macmillan, 1981

Strevens, P, 'On the training of language teachers: A look to the future' in *Topics in Culture Learning 2* (ed) Brislin, Honolulu, Hawaii: East-West Centre, 1974

Widdowson, H G and Davies, E, 'Reading and Writing' in *The Edinburgh Course in Applied Linguistics* (eds Allen and Pit Corder) Vol 3, Oxford: Oxford University Press, 1974

Widdowson, H G, *Stylistics and the Teaching of Literature*, Harlow: Longman, 1975

Widdowson, H G, 'Talking shop' in *English Language Teaching Journal*, Vol 37/1, 1983

Williams, E, *Reading in the Language Classroom*, London: Macmillan, 1984

Further reading

Brumfit, C J (ed) *Language and Literature Teaching: from Practice to Principle*, Oxford: Pergamon, 1985

Burns, C J and McNamara, M G, *Literature: a close study*, London: Macmillan, 1983

Herbert, D and Sturtridge, G, *Simulations*, ELTI The British Council, ELT Guide 2, Windsor: NFER, 1980

King, D and Crerar, T, *A Choice of Words*, Toronto: Oxford University Press, 1969

Melville M, 'Register through Role-play' in *Towards the Creative Teaching of English* (ed) Spaventa, London: Allen and Unwin, 1980

Millar, R and Currie, I, *The Language of Poetry*, London: Heinemann, 1970

Millar, R and Currie, I, *The Language of Prose*, London: Heinemann, 1972

Nuttall, C, *Teaching Reading Skills in a Foreign Language*, London: Heinemann Educational, 1982

Peck, J, *How to Study a Novel*, London: Macmillan, 1983

Protherough, R, *Teaching Literature for Examinations*, Open University Press, 1986

Quirk, R and Widdowson, H G (eds) *English in the World*, Cambridge: Cambridge University Press, 1984

Ramsaran, S, 'Stress, Rhythm and Intonation in the Study of English Literature' in Brumfit (1983), *op. cit.*

Tomlinson, B, 'Using Poetry with mixed ability language classes' in *English Language Teaching Journal* Vol 40/1 1 Jan, 1986

Index